The Chameleon Manager

D1509517

TITLES IN THE

New Skills Portfolio series...

Series Editor: **Linda Holbeche**, Director of Research, Roffey Park Management Institute

Managing More with Less

Joanna Howard

Managing More with Less is an innovative book linking a range of core management skills and re-interpreting them to meet current organizational needs. Aimed at managers in flat organizations, this book shows you how to deal with increasingly scarce resources to maintain a high level of productivity.

0 7506 3698 X • paperback • May 1998

The Chameleon Manager

Brian Clegg

Today's managers are faced with many conflicting demands and situations. This book provides practical ways of achieving the impossible:
- How can you be a generalist and a specialist?
- How can you be an individual expert and a 'connected' team player?
- How can you manage more people with less time and fewer resources and be entrepreneurial at the same time?

Complete with its own website, http://www.cul.co.uk/chameleon, which gives further information and links to other sites.

0 7506 4026 X • paperback • June 1998

Project Skills

Sam Elbeik *and* Mark Thomas

Project Skills describes the best of the accepted project management techniques, taking the guesswork out of deciding which ones to apply at which stage. Elbeik and Thomas present a practical and accessible guide to managing projects of all sizes, not just large-scale ones.

0 7506 3978 4 • paperback • September 1998

Strategic Skills for Team Leaders and Line Managers

Michael Colenso

Strategic Skills for Team Leaders and Line Managers will help line managers and team leaders develop strategy at team or unit level. Increasingly, mid-level managers are required to think and act strategically and contribute extensively to strategy formulation.

0 7506 3982 2 • paperback • September 1998

Honing Your Knowledge Skills

Mariana Funes *and* Nancy Johnson

Honing Your Knowledge Skills looks at how to define knowledge working and identifies the practical skills of knowledge management needed by line managers. This book shows you how to:
- Handle information overload.
- Harness new ideas and become an expert.
- Turn knowledge into action.
- Understand IT resources and knowledge based systems.

0 7506 3699 8 • paperback • September 1998

Managing 'Live' Innovation

Michel Syrett *and* Jean Lammiman

Managing 'Live' Innovation examines the innovation process from the line manager's perspective. This book identifies the skills needed to manage live 'real time' innovation in an environment where products and services are constantly refined, and where customer input is encouraged from an early stage.

0 7506 3700 5 • paperback • September 1998

Available from your local bookshop, or in case of difficulty call
Heinemann Customer Services on (01865) 888000

The Chameleon Manager

Brian Clegg

OXFORD BOSTON JOHANNESBURG MELBOURNE NEW DELHI SINGAPORE

To Gillian, Rebecca and Chelsea

Butterworth-Heinemann
Linacre House, Jordan Hill, Oxford OX2 8DP
225 Wildwood Avenue, Woburn, MA 01801-2041
A division of Reed Educational and Professional Publishing Ltd

℞ A member of the Reed Elsevier plc group

First published 1998

British Library Cataloguing in Publication Data
A catalogue record for this book is available from the British Library

ISBN 0 7506 4026 X

Composition by Genesis Typesetting, Laser Quay, Rochester, Kent
Printed and bound in Great Britain

Contents

Preface

Faced with a world of frantic business change, threatened by the disappearance of job security, what do you do? For some the answer is to keep your head down and wait for early retirement. That's sad enough if you're fifty, but how about forty? Or thirty? Or less? Survival certainly has to be a consideration, but it shouldn't be enough. We all have dreams, goals, things we desperately want to do in a short life. Perhaps it's time to take a different viewpoint.

The Chameleon Manager is about taking that different view, about working your way, not their way. Just as a set of management skills were developed through the twentieth century to cope with the pressures of production line business, so a new set of skills are emerging to manage among worldwide communications, organizational reform and constant, relentless change. *The Chameleon Manager* starts from your dream portfolio, the activities you would be doing if there were no restraints other than your own talents. From there it builds on the skills which are necessary to give your dreams a chance. There are no certainties in this – but then, the only certainty in a conventional job these days is that it isn't going to last for life.

As you move through *The Chameleon Manager* you will find information technology (IT) appearing frequently. Don't let this put you off. Many of the examples come from the world of IT because that's where change is probably fastest, and as a young business it has had to build its own approach, rather than rely on the deadly straitjacket of tradition. You will also find that becoming comfortable with computers and the Internet are essentials for almost every chameleon manager. It's like the transformation a century before when the telephone began to make inroads. Many business people didn't like it; didn't trust it. The only difference is, the rate of change is around twenty times faster.

The Chameleon Manager is about flexibility, about responsiveness – but it's about fun too. Fun and business have rarely been effectively paired. After all, fun's much too touchy-feely, and anyway business is a very serious . . . business. Yet the basis of *The Chameleon Manager* is your dream portfolio – which surely ought to have fun in it somewhere. You have been warned.

Brian Clegg

1 Working *your* way

Preview

- The job for life has gone. We have lost the comfort of stability and need to take control of our own careers.
- A new set of skills are needed to succeed in today's world of business.
- You can choose to survive – to use these skills to keep your current career alive – or you can do more and build on your abilities and aspirations to work *your* way.
- To work your way, you will need to establish a portfolio of activities.
- Working your way is about getting the maximum satisfaction out of your efforts.
- Changing the way you work will require a different attitude to power.
- The Chameleon Manager Web site (http://www.cul.co.uk/chameleon) will help you to keep up to date with the latest skills.

The chameleon manager

Once upon a time there was the job for life. It was possible to join a company as a trainee and spend an entire career within the same, benevolent structure. Your progress was managed for you, bringing out your best qualities to benefit both you and the company. And you lived happily ever after.

That's so obviously a fairy tale. Why, then, is it that so many people still hanker after a job for life? Even if the premise were true, the reality isn't so good. Do you really want big brother managing your career? Can you honestly say with your hand on your heart that you will want the same things for yourself your whole working life? This book will provide you with the skills to take charge.

Chameleons are adaptive, changing appearance to fit with their environment. They're flexible, with independent eyes that can swivel in two different directions at once. As a chameleon manager you will need to be adaptive, to be flexible and more. Even if you aren't a manager in the conventional sense, you can still be a chameleon manager. The way you manage your own work, satisfaction and reward needs a chameleon's talents. Becoming a chameleon manager not only makes sense, it can even make a difference to your (business) survival.

The end of comfort

The attraction of a job for life is security. It's a comfort blanket. Although a degree of risk can be enjoyable, there comes a point where we want someone else to take care of us. Having a job and an income is something few people like to put at risk. Yet bear in mind just how illusory the stability of any job is. It doesn't matter if you are chairman of a vast corporate empire or a self-employed window cleaner, your job is only as safe as your stakeholders will allow it to be. If your board has no faith in you or if the customers don't want your service, that job is going to disappear.

It's a recession when your neighbour loses his job; it's a depression when you lose yours. (Harry S. Truman, thirty-third President of the USA)

There has never been a less stable time for employment. Change is the norm. The business world is in tremendous flux. There is no sign of this slowing down - quite the reverse, everything is speeding up. You only have to compare the speed with which two prime business tools made an impact. The telephone took perhaps thirty years to start providing any real utility. The World Wide Web went from being a limited source of largely useless information to being an interactive shop window for business in around three years.

You have three choices. You can leave your fate to the system. You can wait until your current job is under threat, then start to act. Or you can act now, while you are still in a positive position. Many observers, including business guru Charles Handy, refer to the need to move businesses on while they are still in the ascendancy. By using the image of a sigmoid curve, Handy says that the time to change the business is not when it begins to fail, but while it is still strong. 'Don't change it if it ain't broke' no longer applies. It is going to break – the trick is to change before it does. Similarly with your career, to get on to the next curve, to start the next ascent, it's best to make the move while things are still going well – at point A, not point B. Don't wait for the company to force the change. Take charge.

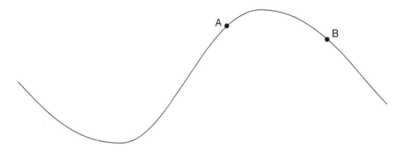

MORE INFO . . .

Charles Handy in *The Empty Raincoat* (Hutchinson, 1994) describes the paradoxes that we face in modern business and a set of 'pathways through the paradox' including the sigmoid curve.

Solutions

Who's to say that you haven't already achieved the right moves? It is quite possible, but for most people it is unlikely. However fulfilling your current job is, it is likely to be only a subset of what you really desire. With only one attempt at life, do you want to look back and think 'if only . . .' or do you want to take a shot at your dreams?

There are two levels at which you can use this book. The first is survival. To be able to carry on down the path you have already started, you will need to broaden your scope to take on the new skills that are driving businesses into the twenty-first century. The second is control. Taking these new skills, adding them to your own unique abilities and aspirations, and developing a career that is oriented not to the way a particular company wants to use you, but to the way you want to be. That's how you should use it. It's not going to be easy to make the break, but it will be a lot more fun than surviving. If surviving is all you can manage, at least that's better than the alternative.

Living is my job and my art. (Montaigne, sixteenth-century French moralist and essayist)

The lottery directive

Activities are an essential part of The Chameleon Manager. *This can be a problem because it's very tempting not to bother with the exercises in a book but to skip over them, thinking briefly about what you would have done if you had the time and the inclination. Unfortunately, this approach will not work here. The activities are there to help you establish yourself as a chameleon manager. Without undertaking them you will not succeed.*

We will be looking further into your abilities and aspirations in the next chapter. For the moment, let's try a simple activity to assess how good a match you already are to your perfect job.

Step 1   *Jot down the main activities that you currently perform, both at work and for recreation. Set the level of detail so that you list around a dozen of them.*

Step 2   *Imagine that you have won the jackpot in a major lottery. You now have enough money to live comfortably for the rest of your life. Take a moment to luxuriate in the possibilities.*

Step 3 *Draw up two columns on a sheet of paper, headed 'Continue' and 'Drop'. Sort your activities into these columns. Which would you continue to do even if you had no need to earn money? Which would you drop like a hot brick?*

Step 4 *Estimate how much time a week is spent on the activities in the 'Drop' column. Multiply that up for a year.*

Result *We aren't going to do anything more with this list yet. Just be aware of how much time you are wasting on things you don't want to do. Later we will find ways to change this.*

New skills

The skills we are going to develop are particularly oriented to the fast-changing, frightening world that business has become:

- **Managing constant change** – the impact of change on business has become a cliché. Managing change is more than coming to enjoy change yourself. You have to be able to manage it for others, to help them to come to terms with it and, if not love it, at least to appreciate the need for it.

- **Becoming an expert** – there was a time when you could get by with being average. You were measured on inputs – did you turn up for work on time, how did you dress – rather than on outputs – what was the quality of your work, did you meet the desired objectives. Now output is king. You have to become an expert, and be recognized as such.

- **Managing network relationships** – whether you work in a busy office, or on a croft in the Scottish Isles, networks are essential to modern business survival. Your reports, bosses, co-workers, customers, potential customers . . . there is a spider's web of influence that can make the difference between no job at all and success. It's up to you to manage this network, however divorced from your 'real job' it may seem.

- **Managing more with less** – the last ten to twenty years have seen an increasing requirement to do more with less: greater productivity, more cost saving, working smart. This requirement is not going to go away. What is happening, though, is a growing awareness that cost isn't the sole driver, and that the new generation of managing more with less is as much about increasing quality as it is about shaving off another penny.

- **Turning stress into creative success** – stress is a killer that plagues modern society, yet total absence of stress is equally undesirable. You need to be able to take your drives and problems and feed them into your work, deflecting the pressure so that it adds power to your output rather than crushing you.

- **Managing innovation** – there's a common fallacy that creativity can be left to special, 'creative' people while the rest of us manage without it. The trouble is, everyone agrees that innovation is the prime driver for business success in a fast-changing world. You need to find ways to be more creative yourself and to manage the creativity of others.

- **Honing your knowledge skills** – there has never been more information available, and it has never been more necessary to structure the morass of data and turn it into workable knowledge. The need for learning parallels the development of new sources of information like the World Wide Web. Knowledge runs alongside innovation in keeping business afloat.

- **Managing team dynamics** – teamwork is the order of the day. Large companies are dividing into smaller units. Start-up business are springing up everywhere. At the same time, the production line approach is giving way to greater use of production teams, giving individuals a wider remit, a more interesting job and more commitments. Whether it's dealing with your own team or interacting with many other companies, team dynamics are a key to success.

- **Total management skills** – the new manager, the total manager, has to take on a much broader role. Where once it was enough to issue instructions, now there is a requirement for leadership. Where a manager's concern for staff was mostly about timekeeping and completing tasks, now it has to include empowerment and fun. The overall nature of management is changing quickly – individual managers have to change with it by developing total management skills.

This isn't a cookbook. You won't find a chapter on each item listed above. Instead this book will guide you through the process of developing yourself to work *your* way, bringing on board the new skills as they become appropriate.

Take two minutes to look back over these skills. Are there areas where you could make improvements? Are they relevant to your current job? Are they relevant to your future?

Ability and aspirations

Before you can take on change there are two things that have to be established. What abilities you already have, and where you want to be going. Change for its own sake is a waste of energy. The main thing here is to focus your effort on making changes that move you towards your goals.

When you have established what you are good at, and what you would like to be doing, there will be a number of obstacles in the way. The skills that are introduced in this book will help overcome those obstacles, but in the end they will only be overcome if you have a burning desire to make it all happen.

Your portfolio

Few of us are so perfectly focused that a single task is our only possibility and our only desire; to be honest, such a person sounds rather boring. You can regard the range of activities you might undertake as your personal portfolio, rather like a shareholder might have a portfolio of shares.

How you deal with your portfolio will differ hugely from individual to individual. For many it will be necessary to focus on one aspect of the portfolio at a time. Other activities might be introduced in parallel, but in a compartmentalized way. So, for example, you might have one activity as your current job, another as a hobby and another that you plan to be your job in five years time. A next stage might be to have a portfolio of tasks, but still within a single organization: working on task forces, having secondary responsibilities and so forth. Others go beyond this and work with a simultaneous portfolio. Here several jobs are taken on simultaneously. This could be in a traditional work format by having several part-time jobs, but most often it involves self-employment or starting your own company and providing different roles and services at different times.

The writer and creative consultant

My own development of a portfolio went from compartmentalized to simultaneous. For seventeen years I worked in a corporate environment. To begin with this was enough. Later, various other threads came in as spare-time activities. I began writing for magazines and also wrote some fiction. Through training at work, I started to use creativity techniques in my work environment, doing a small amount of consultancy and training within the company, building a portfolio beyond my specific job description.

When I made the break, it was to build a complex simultaneous portfolio. At the time of writing I am working on two books (both commissioned), have a novel under way, write reviews, columns and features for two published IT magazines and a lifestyle magazine on the World Wide Web, provide business creativity consultancy, do a small amount of visual programming, am developing some creativity software and am working on some intranet pages to put across IT innovation to a corporate. All this is active work, with other time given to administration, developing my Web site and looking for new work for the future. It sounds hectic – it is. But it's also the most enjoyable work I've ever done.

The simultaneous portfolio has pros and cons. It offers the best fit to your aspirations – you are likely to get more out of it personally than through any other approach. There's the opportunity for freshness. When you've had enough of a particular task, you can switch to a totally different role for a while. As long as these switches are significant they will actually improve your productivity; changing to a whole new activity acts almost like a rest. On the negative side, though, you have to take personal charge of everything. You are responsible for your time. You are responsible for getting the right mix of tasks and maintaining them. You will be faced with a complex balancing act, as some tasks will usually be better paid than others. It is not a trivial step to take.

Creative challenge

Managing a portfolio requires a more creative approach to working. In this quick activity you will have an opportunity to take a creative view of a problem.

Step 1   *Get comfortable. Make sure that you are relaxed. If you are sitting at your desk, turn away. If you are wearing a tie, loosen it. Now take a very brief physical exercise. This will help you to react more creatively. Stand up and stretch as high as you can, holding the stretch for a few seconds. If you are in an environment where this makes you look strange, don't worry – do it anyway. Pretend you are reaching for something.*

Step 2   *Imagine that you are in London. You need to get to New York. Your only resource is a matchbox. How are you going to do it?*

Step 3   *If you haven't spent a couple of minutes trying, go back to Step 2 and have a go before reading on. No cheating.*

Step 4   *In fact there are many ways you could do this. The matchbox could be made of gold – sell it and buy a plane ticket. Or it could be a huge wooden matchbox in which you could row across the Atlantic. Or it could actually be a 747, with the matches stored inside it. Or it could be a rare Matchbox toy, which you could trade with a* *collector for a ticket. Etc., etc. This might seem disappointing as a solution. It's cheating, which is pretty rich considering that I specifically instructed you not to cheat. Yet all that was cheated is the set of assumptions you made. Time after time, in looking at your career, in developing your skills, in working, you make assumptions that aren't necessarily valid.*

Result *If you got an answer, great. If you didn't, don't worry. The point of the activity is to be aware of how much we are conditioned by habit and what has happened in the past. The new skills you will be taking on will help you to work differently, and that requires an ability to break out from the way things have always been done.*

Note also Step 1. If your job is largely sedentary, be aware of the need for physical change at regular intervals to keep your body and mind active.

Power tools

Changing the way you work, taking on a personal portfolio, will require a different attitude to power. Your immediate reaction may be 'so what?' After all, you aren't a mega-lomaniac, driven by the search for power like all those bad guys in the Bond films, or even, perhaps, one or two chief executive officers (CEOs) you could name. Yet consider what power is. It is, in essence, the ability to make something happen. And it is rare that even the most high-minded aspirations will not have some aspects of power, given this definition.

It's worth taking a moment to consider what power is based on. In the late 1950s, French and Raven defined a number of possible sources of social power:

- **Reward power** - power based on the ability or the perceived ability to reward actions. The carrot part of the classical carrot and stick - pay rises, bonuses, promotion, training, jollies (business trips to desirable locations) and the like.

- **Coercive power** – the stick element. The ability to punish: holding back any of the above, sacking, humiliation. Between them, reward and coercive power represent traditional management weaponry.

- **Referent power** – a much more subtle concept, referent power is based on the ability to make others want to be like you. Leading by example often generates referent power, which is a much more valuable tool than reward or coercion when dealing with technical staff who are likely to be unimpressed by conventional authority, but strongly influenced by technical superiority. The power of the charismatic, referent power, despite its subtlety can be immensely strong.

- **Expert power** – power based on real or perceived specialist knowledge. Expert power is at its rawest where, for example, a doctor takes charge in a medical emergency. Very much in the ascendancy, expert power is the power of the consultant, brought in from outside the organization for his or her particular knowledge.

- **Legitimate power** – power based on structure and tradition. The power of a Member of Parliament, a police officer, a company director. Note that this is quite distinct from reward and coercion. A director will generally have these powers as well, but legitimate power comes from the assumption that such people have power purely as a result of their rank and status. This is the element of power which is most questioned at present.

MORE INFO . . .

See French and Raven's article 'The sources of social power', in *Studies in Social Power* (University of Michigan Press, 1959), edited by D. Cartwright.

Although French and Raven's study is almost forty years old, the approach is very valuable for understanding the change that takes place when becoming a chameleon manager. Traditionally your power was based on reward and coercion (with perhaps some degree of legitimacy). In building your own portfolio you are trying to work *your* way, not *theirs*.

This means losing the power given to you by structure and position. Instead referent and expert power become much more important. In this book you will find a great deal more about these; about selling yourself and developing leadership skills – generating referent power – and about building knowledge and expertise – expert power. Driven by your new skills, these two will form the power base to make your portfolio a reality.

Walking the Web

Any book is out of date as soon as it goes to print – and never more so than in such a fast-changing environment. The Chameleon Manager Web site (http://www.cul.co.uk/ chameleon) is available to expand the benefits you get from this book. If you have access to the World Wide Web, use it to check on new information – and to feed back your own experience. If you don't have access, I will be discussing how to get it in a couple of chapters' time. The Internet, and specifically the Web, is no longer an optional business tool.

Working *your* way

key concept

No more job for life.
Your personal portfolio.
Surviving or growing.
Working *your* way.
Referent and expert power.

Whichever approach you decide to take, your goal is to work *your* way, not *their* way. It may be that you move into this gradually, perhaps building your portfolio by taking on one of your aspirations as a hobby and maintaining your current day job. Such an approach is fine, as long as you are genuinely moving to take control of your working life. Sometimes the choice is not left up to you. Redundancy is not the best place to start the rest of your career, but it may be your only option.

You may be further along the sigmoid curve than you realize. If this is the case you have further to go. You may have to take on a temporary job to keep going while you manage the transformation. But never lose sight of the goal.

With this requirement in mind, the next step is to establish exactly what your dream portfolio would be.

2 Mapping your employment dreams

key concept Managing with constant change, becoming an internal expert.

Preview

- To make use of the new skills you first need to know what your existing skills are and what you would like to be doing with them.
- Establishing your existing skills, in work and outside it.
- Building a picture of your ideal portfolio.
- Establishing the obstacles to making it happen.
- Putting together a plan to overcome the obstacles.

What have you got; what do you want?

Before you can absorb and use new skills, it is sensible to clarify your goals. Where do you want to get to in life and in your career as a result of taking on new skills? To understand the journey, you also need to know where you are starting from. Of course you know already, you've got a curriculum vitae (CV) . . . but there's a lot more to it than that. This chapter is mostly comprised of activities, because it's about discovering your own position.

Mind maps or paper scraps

Building up a view of your abilities and desires involves exploring a relatively unstructured area, so it's worth having a tool to help. As you think more about your experience and wishes, new ideas will pop up in different areas. Try one of these simple techniques to help pull things together.

Outlining

If you are comfortable typing ideas directly into a computer, you might like to use the outliner found in most word processors and presentation graphics software. This enables you to have a flexible set of headings and slot thoughts under them as you proceed. If you haven't got a word processor, any text-handling software, however basic, will allow you to pop thoughts into the appropriate place as you go along.

Paper scraps

If you aren't comfortable with a computer, try paper scraps. At its simplest this involves using a large, clear table and a set of small pieces of paper or file cards. You can physically rearrange the ideas on the table. If you've got a whiteboard and Post-it notes these are even better, as they provide the same flexibility as paper or cards, but make it easier to obtain an overview. What's more, you can structure the notes, and they won't blow away if someone opens the door too quickly.

Mind maps

The most sophisticated approach, though still simple to use, is the mind map. There are many variants on the concept of drawing a picture of a set of linked concepts or ideas, but the specific term 'mind-mapping' was devised by Tony Buzan.

MORE INFO . . .

For everything you ever wanted to know about mind maps, see Tony and Barry Buzan's, *The Mind Map Book* (BBC Books, 1993).

Take a blank sheet of paper and turn it on its side in a landscape position. In the centre of the sheet, draw a circle and write in it the main idea you are considering. It might be your skills. From this centre draw a set of thick branches, each representing a major aspect. They might be the main areas covered by your skills. Write a very short description of the item on top of each branch. You can then add twigs that break these down into more detail. Use key words as much as possible – they keep the information input to a minimum.

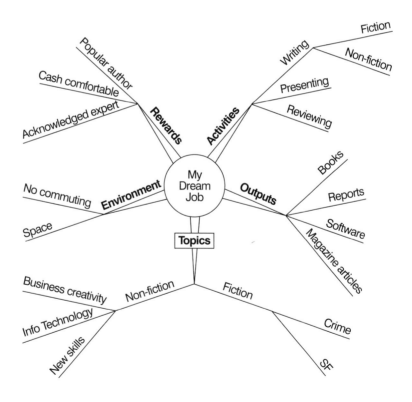

The great thing about a mind map is that it can be developed totally flexibly, adding information organically as it springs to mind. It is supposed to be structured in a way that reflects the way the mind stores information, so once it is presented in this form you may find it easier to overview and digest. Whether or not this is the case, it's a great way of making structured notes.

NOTE . . .

If you like using computers but want to have a mind map, there are a number of products on the market to help. VisiMap from CoCo Systems (http://www.coco.co.uk) and MindMan from MindMan Inc (http://mindman.com) are good examples. Check out the Chameleon Manager Web site (http://www.cul.co.uk/chameleon) for more suggestions.

The talent list

A necessary input is what you are good at, or feel you could be good at with practice or training.

Step 1   *Think through what you do at work. What do you feel you do particularly well? Don't be modest, be honest. Is there anything that other people have complimented you on, either informally or through some form of assessment? Jot down one-word, or at most one-line, items.*

Step 2   *Think through your life outside work. What do you do well in your spare time? With your family? In any activities you undertake? Add them to the list. Don't segregate these items from the others: they all form part of your skill set.*

Step 3   *Look back at your life before your present job. Were there activities at school, at college, in other jobs, which you have had some particular ability in? Add them to the list; perhaps they're rusty, but they may still be useful.*

Step 4   *Speculate. Are there things that you've never done, but you think you would be good at? This isn't wish fulfilment or fantasy – these should be things that you would have a reasonable chance to be* *good at, but haven't tried. It's more likely to be chicken farming or computer programming than playing football for England.*

Step 5 *Structure your list. See if there are any common threads.*

Result *You now should have a clearer idea of the abilities that you will be bringing into the arena. You will use these later to test the feasibility of your dream activities, and to help set your direction.*

We are about to enter a concentrated period of looking forward. Take a moment to look back over your career so far and pick out one thing that you are particularly proud of. Building your personal portfolio isn't about knocking your achievements to date – don't forget them.

The dream picture

Now for the fun part. We are going to use a number of activities to pull together a picture of what you would really like to be doing. Know that already? Perhaps, but until you think about it in a structured way, the chances are you haven't really explored your desires. Don't feel you have to use all the following activities, but try more than one. Whichever you use, do also try the first activity, loads-a-money.

Loads-a-money

In the first chapter you looked at which activities you would still undertake and which you would drop if you won a major lottery. Now you are going to take this one stage further. If you've already done the lottery directive activity, get your output now.

NOTE . . .

See page 4 for the lottery directive activity.

If you haven't, skip back and do it now.

MAPPING YOUR EMPLOYMENT DREAMS

Step 1   *Take your activities list, divided into 'Continue' and 'Drop' columns. Add a third column: 'New'.*

Step 2   *Remember your position. You need never work again. You have enough money on which to live comfortably for the rest of your life. Which activities that you don't do now would you add? Don't be practical. Just write down what you would really like to do, however infeasible it is.*

Step 3   *Bring your skills list alongside. Check out the practicality of your 'New' column against this. Don't cross anything off, but highlight those which are a particularly good fit or a particularly bad fit. For instance, if you've written 'play football for England' and you have two left feet, it's a bad fit. If you've written 'teach adults' and you are good at communicating, it's a good fit.*

Result   *You've now got a list of activities you'd like to do. Some you do at present, others are new. Keep it somewhere within easy reach – you'll need it again.*

Desert island

Imagine that you have been stranded on a desert island. There's plenty of food and drink, comfortable shelter and you have rescued from the wreck some tools, a pile of paper and pencils. You know that in ten years' time there will be another boat – but for the next ten years you will be on your own. What will you do? Is there anything you can learn from your experience on the island?

Processed life

Most of the dream picture activities lack structure. If you like a structured approach, this might be the activity for you. But do try a couple of the others as well.

Step 1   *What is ideal work about for you? What categories can aspects of it be split into? The mind map below shows one possible categorization – activities, outputs, rewards, topics and environment. Another set might be people, markets, products, finance, operating, information – the category set of a typical old-style, vertically organized company. The important thing in establishing your categories is that you are comfortable with them and they don't compromise you by forcing you to be practicable. This is about establishing your ideal job, not something you can walk into tomorrow. At this stage, neither opportunities nor obstacles should be categories.*

Step 2   *Under each category, list anything that appeals to you. Try to be clear that anything you add really would be desirable. It's tempting to put 'be a billionaire', but for most of us that much money would be unusable and a burden (do you always want to have to be protected against kidnappers wherever you go? Do you want your children to need bodyguards?). If having money is important to you, try to judge what your comfort level is.*

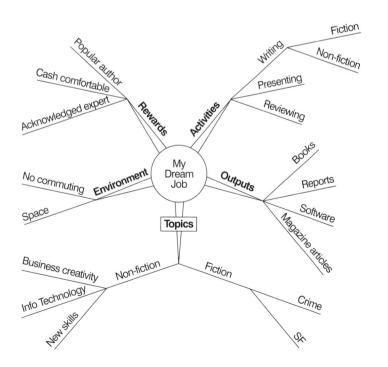

Step 3   *Continue this until you run out of ideas. You can go down multiple levels. You may well find that a mind map is the best way to lay out the information.*

Step 4   *Collate. You will probably need to combine points from under different topics to come up with the combinations that appeal.*

Look at the mind map again. Some of the headings combine to establish my desired outcome. I could combine writing books with practically any of the topics headings, but I don't particularly want to review magazine articles. I might want to be an acknowledged expert in my non-fiction topics, but not particularly in the fictional ones.

Result   *The structured approach is most likely to generate possibilities that are relatively close to your current occupation. Remember to consider what you do out of work, and what you'd like to do too. The output of this exercise, combined with another, will give you a good picture.*

A perfect day

A very simple activity that is surprisingly good at pulling out extra requirements, particularly in the space around your work. No one can work effectively and constantly for all their waking hours.

Step 1   *Think through your ideal working day, from waking in the morning to going to bed. Write a detailed schedule. Go into fairly painful detail. For example:*

- *Get up around eight.*
- *Make a cup of coffee and go back to bed.*
- *Read for half an hour while I drink my coffee.*
- *Get dressed.*
- *Etc.*

Step 2   *Distil from your picture of your perfect day the activities that you would really like to be doing. Note also the approximate timings.*

Result   *The perfect day will have provided a different slant and new activities for your list.*

Losing your best staff

If you have staff working for you, the dream picture can present you with a real dilemma. When I first started to plot out my own future, I got so excited about it that I wanted everyone else to benefit. So I had a series of career sessions with my staff and got them to do the same. The outcome was that two of my best people left the company sooner than they otherwise would have. They have both had exciting and rewarding careers since (though very different: one heads a development group in Microsoft's Seattle headquarters, the other works from home in Aylesbury).

There is no doubt at all that from their point of view this was a beneficial process. What about for me, as a manager, and for the company, though? It's a painful lesson, but there is no doubt that it pays to put your staff's development above your own requirements, otherwise you are going to hold someone back who should be doing better things. If you don't, the only outcome is likely to be their bitterness and collapse of performance.

Couldn't you simply keep them in ignorance? They will find out eventually, but why hurry the day? The last thing you want to do is push such people out, but equally you owe them more for all the great work they've done for you in the past than to keep them in the dark. Anyway, who knows, you might end up working for them one day. Best to keep them sweet.

Skill and fun

This is a halfway exercise between structured and fantasy.

Step 1   *Take your skills list. If you haven't already written one, go back to page 18 and put one together.*

Step 2   *Alongside the skills put a second column headed 'Fun'. Write down everything you consider to be fun.*

Step 3   *Look for combinations. Are there ways you can make use of one or more of your skills and do something you consider fun? Make as many combinations as you can. Some will be fairly bizarre. Don't worry about this.*

Result   *Your fun/skill combinations should contain the seeds of some activities. Even if you've got something that is apparently impractical (not to mention illegal), it might inspire you to think of something that is achievable.*

Consolidation

Whichever approach you have taken, you should be able to pull together a reasonable picture of your ideal working life. Try to describe this in a few, short, key sentences. This is your dream portfolio, the activity collection that you would like to be doing if it were possible. Now it's up to you to make it happen.

The obstacle map

We combat obstacles in order to get repose, and, when got, the repose is insupportable. (Henry Brooks Adams, nineteenth-century US writer)

It's not enough to know what you want. You've also got to be able to get there. For some of us, the ideal is quite close to reality. For others it is unbelievably far away. It may be that you can only ever achieve part of your dream portfolio, but this doesn't make it any less worth trying. Generally there will be obstacles that prevent you from achieving your goals. This activity helps establish what these obstacles are.

Step 1   *Find a blank piece of paper. A4 will do, but a bigger size would be better. Draw out a basic obstacle map, as illustrated.*

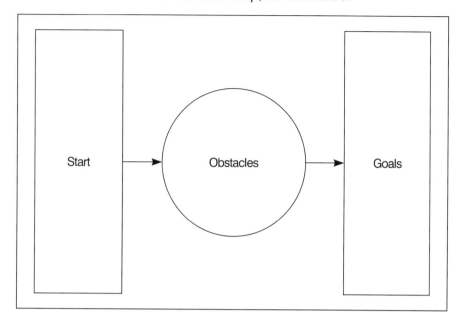

Step 2   *In the 'Goals' box, list the output of your dream portfolio activities.*

Step 3   *In the 'Start' box, describe your current position in similar short phrases.*

Step 4   *In the 'Obstacles' box, list what is getting in the way. What would you have to overcome to move from your current state to your ideal work?*

Result   *By bringing together your present state and your desires, the obstacle map helps clarify the blockages that are preventing you from achieving your goals.*

Overcoming your obstacles

The rest of this book introduces skills with two aims in mind. They will help you to perform a new role, but they will also help to overcome the obstacles that lie between your current position and your desires. Some, like the creativity techniques in Chapter 5, are explicit problem-solving skills. Others will be laying the foundations for the sort of business roles that are increasingly required.

By making your obstacles explicit, you have effectively added to your list of goals. Overcoming those obstacles should be a driver for your activity from now on. Many of the obstacles are probably not under your direct control. However, it is still useful to set yourself milestones for overcoming them, if only to make sure that they remain on your agenda and aren't swept out of the way by the constant flood of everyday activity. There's nothing easier to put off than an activity that is building something with long-term rewards. But if you are not careful, you can spend the rest of your life putting it off, and never come near to fulfilling your dreams.

Ready for action

Present and future skills.
Your dream portfolio.
Goals and obstacles.

By now you should have a fair idea of what you'd ideally like to do, where you are now, and what the obstacles are to making it happen. The remaining chapters will provide mechanisms for overcoming those obstacles and achieving your goals. However your portfolio develops, whether it's into simultaneous tasks or a reasonably linear career, you will need to find work. Even if you are well established in a strong company, this is ultimately your responsibility. After all, there are few people, at least in Western cultures, who would be happy to sit back and let someone else decide how their personal life develops; it's strange that so many expect the company to manage their careers.

3 Finding work

Managing with constant change, managing network relationships.

Preview

- Building your personal portfolio implies finding new roles and tasks.
- Expanding your internal role, or moonlighting.
- In a conventional career, opportunities must be tracked, the CV kept polished and the wider world kept under constant consideration.
- With a simultaneous portfolio there is a constant need to review customers and possible tasks.
- Whichever approach is taken, it is essential to have a good network of contacts and to market yourself.
- Traditional vehicles include trade publications, general press, your address book and task list.
- New vehicles are provided by the Internet and particularly the World Wide Web.

Walking before you can run

If you've decided that you want to continue with a conventional career, be very aware of what you are doing. Such roles are in decline. We have already reached a state where full-time conventional jobs are in the minority, and they continue to disappear. If you currently have a conventional job, it makes a lot of sense to dip your toe in the water of flexibility, to expand your portfolio without actually cutting adrift from your old job. The advantages are that you get a chance to find your feet without taking too much of a risk. In the end you may well have to make the leap (or be pushed), but for the moment you can dabble in aspects of your dream employment with limited risk.

You will note that I don't say you can do it without any risk whatsoever. It's hard to find any activity that is risk free, and it is certainly true that putting your head over the parapet brings with it a degree of exposure. Some bosses may be inclined to see your moves to broaden yourself as frivolous, diluting or even personally threatening. There's no easy answer to this one.

The safest approach is when you can take on a new activity within your existing work framework that is regarded as safe or worthy. You can see the sort of things that might be appropriate in internal training manuals. Consultancy skills, facilitation, communication skills, business creativity and so forth. The challenge is, having established the direction, to get something going within the company as a result of it.

The jester

Paul had worked in practically every department in British Airways, including several challenging senior management posts. He developed particular skills around consulting and facilitation. The conventional move might have been to some form of internal consultant role, but such individuals are constrained by the need to be asked in. Instead, Paul conceived of the role of corporate jester. Just as the medieval jester was the only one who could say what he really thought to the king, the corporate jester's job would be to stir up senior management, suggesting ways of doing things differently.

The job was sanctioned by BA's then chief executive, Sir Colin Marshall. For fourteen months, Paul undertook a role that was a radical shift away from anything he had ever undertaken before – and a major step towards his ideal portfolio. He left the airline in 1997 when the opportunity arose to add another element – developing a maze and countryside centre in rural Wales. Paul maintains the jester role as an external consultant with a number of companies.

The maze and countryside centre, jointly developed with his wife, illustrates two other lessons of the portfolio. The centre was at least ten years from initial conception to opening. Dream activities will often be a long time in the development. And where Paul's old career was traditionally solo, he now works much more in partnership with his wife. New ways of working are bringing back the family firm.

To develop a new skill practically, you need to make time for a personal project. Find some aspect of your part of the business that could be improved by doing things your new way. Find an opportunity to make this particular ability useful and visible; useful to increase demand, visible because you want to be known as the expert in whatever the skill is (this is where your head goes over the parapet). That way you will be well placed if an opportunity arises to make this activity more central to your job – or to give up your current portfolio and take a step in another direction.

That's fine if your dreams fit within the confines of your current workplace, but what if it's for something completely different? It is not unusual that a mid-life crisis results in a major change of direction. Around the age of forty seems to be a natural time to reassess your portfolio. Yet I am suggesting this is something you should be doing annually. One of the results of this will be people across a range of ages realizing just how far they are from what they'd really like to be doing – plenty more people looking for a new path.

The only way to bridge the gap, to avoid jumping too soon, is moonlighting. Doing more than one job. 'What's new?' many women would say. Absolutely, but business culture has not traditionally been tolerant of moonlighting. The theory is that your principal work activity will suffer because you are doing something else on the side. There's something mildly hypocritical about the fact that many of the strongest exponents of this belief put a huge amount of effort into developing their golf – but, of course, that's different.

Moonlighting has traditionally been frowned upon for two reasons. One is a tendency to use company resources for personal gain – copying on the company photocopier, using the company phone. The other is that it has often involved extra manual work for an employee who already has an exhausting job, resulting in poor performance and excessive sick leave. The first of these is a dangerous trap that must be avoided. You must be squeaky clean about your moonlighting. The second is of less significance. Your moonlighting may be desk-bound or physical, but it is unlikely to overwhelm you.

The other difference from conventional moonlighting is that our version is not about money. A second job was traditionally taken on to make ends meet. This new generation of moonlighting is about developing skills and a market before swinging into a new way of working. Probably the best model for this sort of moonlighting is a hobby. Invest your alternative activity with the sort of time and effort that are traditionally poured into a hobby. Of course, that might involve putting some other activity aside (unless your moonlighting already was a hobby). But the experience will be worth it.

If the activity is fairly self-contained, you can probably do it without any discussion with your employer. For instance, if your dream is to become an apiarist or a goldsmith you are unlikely to meet with any objections. However a higher profile activity, especially one which is obviously paid, carries more risk. Most contracts have clauses preventing individuals drawing a salary from someone else, and ensuring that any fee-earning activity is made known. Often the requirement is to notify an administrator. This should be done in as low key a manner as possible, minimizing any possible response from the company. Dealing with an unsympathetic boss can be harder, yet if your dream means anything to you, it will be worth it.

How would you feel if you found out someone working for you was moonlighting? What would you say to them? Does this have any implications for you?

Keeping the CV polished

A CV or résumé is not a document most of us think about much. It's often the oldest file on your personal computer. You dig it out when times are hard, or you're bored, but generally it doesn't see the light of day. In fact there's something rather unpleasant about someone who spends all their time reading their CV. They're either obsessed with their career or simply narcissistic. It is certainly not necessary to make your CV daily reading. On the other hand, you never know when you'll need it.

Why not tie a brief update of your CV into the development of your personal portfolio? It's not the same thing, of course. A CV is essentially backward looking, while a portfolio looks forward. Yet they have enough in common to make it a sensible combination. While you are at it, check out the look and feel of your CV. Bear in mind that whoever reads it is liable to have read a good number of them. You can immediately improve the chances that yours gets some attention by making it short, readable and well presented. No one wants to plough through a twelve-page screed in eight-point capitals. Don't be tempted, though, to go too far the other way and either skimp on important content or make it so flashy that it's distracting. In the world of CVs there's a fine line between beautifully presented and overblown.

Media CVs

Step 1   *Make sure your current CV is up to date. Read it through. Have it ready as a reference.*

Step 2   *Imagine your CV was going to be published in a tabloid newspaper. Spend five minutes putting together the tabloid version.*

Step 3   *Imagine turning your CV into a thirty-second television advertisement for you. Spend five minutes roughing out the script.*

FINDING WORK

Step 4   *Imagine your CV is being put together by the editor of a trendy fashion magazine. Don't worry too much about the content, but what would it look like?*

Result   *There's a creativity technique called 'someone else's view' where you take on a different persona to get a new look at a problem. There's no suggestion that you should scrap your current CV and replace it with one of the three above, but each can teach you something about improving your CV. The tabloid CV has to put information across briefly, and needs to be a simple, easy read. How readable is your current CV? The television advertisement has to be slick, sexy (or funny) and compact. It would make a change for a CV. Fashion magazines use layout to achieve a purpose. Does your CV look like a magazine page or an obituary?*

Watching your company

If you are currently with a company, how much attention do you pay to it? Do you know your share price, and how it has moved? How about last year's results? It's a pain if (like me) you find such information intensely boring, but knowing what your company is doing is essential if you are to make best use of it in developing yourself. Apart from watching what the company is doing in general, there are a number of key factors to consider.

Bearing in mind that your aim is to change, you should watch for change within your company. Reorganizations, special task forces, one-off projects are all replete with opportunities to get involved and take a change of direction. As usual, there's an element of risk. Many large companies don't know how to handle staff who are on special projects. When the project is completed, it is equally likely that members of the project team will step into a new and exciting job, or be sidelined into a sort of limbo with no real place to go. Yet getting involved in such projects is a great way to provide the experience for broadening your portfolio.

Always have your current portfolio goals and obstacles in mind when you are looking at the in-house magazine or whatever else is used to communicate what's going on. Look for the opportunity to take a step in the right direction by getting involved in something. It may even be a company social or environmental activity, but whatever it involves, your company is a rich source of potential development.

Watching the world

If a single company has so much potential, think what the rest of the world can offer. The advantage of the company is that you are already an insider, but of course it isn't the only place where this is true. Within your town or village, within whatever social structures you are part of, there will be possible applications of your dream activities. Make sure you know what's going on. Beyond that, you will have to be more assertive and, most of all, keep your eyes open. Whether you are watching the news or travelling on the tube, you are being bombarded with images and activity. Always keep your dream picture at the back of your mind in case anything you see triggers a possibility.

Driven by a bus

Dean Hill runs workshops for the performing arts in the USA. His entire direction was influenced by a poster seen on the side of a bus in Cleveland, Ohio. It read: 'The only true art is art which affects the quality of the day'. This sparked his thinking about where he should be going and what he should be doing in a way that has shaped the rest of his life.

So far we have used a passive approach; the next few sections will look at more active ways of finding activities that fit your desired pattern.

The customer net

Whether you remain employed by someone else or develop your own portfolio business, you will have customers. Within a company, your customers will typically be your boss and those your work directly effects. If you are running your own business your customers will be more explicit. Early in the game they are likely to be contacts you made while in a previous job. Your main customer may even be your previous employer. But over time your customer base will grow. In either case, these people are very important to you. It's tedious, I know, but it is essential that you build up a basic customer database. This need not be an all-singing, all-dancing computer system. It can be an address book and diary. The important thing is that you understand when you should next contact a key customer, and that you know a bit about them.

If you are working from home (more on this later) it is doubly important that you keep your eye on your customers. One of the magazines I write for goes through editors pretty quickly (I'm on my fifth). I make a point of meeting the editor in person reasonably soon after they take the job, and approximately six-monthly after that. All the business we do could be conducted over the phone, by e-mail and by post, but there's something very reassuring about having met someone. It makes the relationship more personal. And this works both ways. Remember you are dependent on your customers' goodwill for survival. They are less likely to drop you without a thought if you aren't just a name on a piece of paper. That's not to say they won't drop you anyway, just that you are improving your chances.

In the same way that you keep an eye on your company, you need to keep an eye on your customers' activities. You never know when a new requirement they have will give you the opportunity to point out 'Oh, really? That's amazing, because that's something I'm doing a lot of these days . . .'.

Top customers

Step 1   *Think through your current customers, and anyone you've already identified as possible customers for your portfolio. Try to pick out seven to ten who are most important to you as an individual. Remember, we're thinking of bosses, employers, clients, anyone responsible for starting you on an activity.*

Step 2   *For each of your top people note down when you last saw them, when you are next due to see them, what they are currently expecting from you and what you want from them.*

Step 3   *For each of your top people, note down what you know about them on a personal basis. Do they have a family? How do they take their coffee?*

Result   *This activity should provide you with a picture of the state of your customer database. If you couldn't give much of an answer to Step 3, you need to find out more information soon. If you couldn't give much of an answer to Step 2, you are in deep trouble, and need to get working on it very quickly. If you couldn't identify more than one or two customers, you had better have a good personal network through which to obtain some more.*

The personal network

Your customers are part of the ever-present invisible web that is your personal network. We all have a four-dimensional spider's web surrounding us, linking to hundreds of other people across space and time. It's not a neat, organized table; it's a crazy, circumstance-driven array. As soon as you begin to interact with other people you develop networks – playgroup or nursery, schools, universities, workplace, neighbours, family, friends, clubs and organizations – whatever you do, you are adding to this immense web, or net.

When you are looking for activities that will bring you closer to your ideal, your network is an incredibly powerful resource. At one time it was the 'old boys' network' that seemed to run Britain. Whether your most important links go as far back as school, or are the ones you make through your business, these individuals are essential stepping-stones to achieving your goals. This sounds rather unpleasant. Few of us actually enjoy walking over someone else. And if you view your network solely as a way to benefit from others, it will certainly shrivel up and die. The success of the old boys' network and many others like it is mutual support. Yes, you are going to use other people, but with their knowledge, and with the understanding that they can use you too.

In the previous section, I suggested we all need a customer database. In fact, what we need is a network database. Something more than an address book that lets us keep track of who is who, who we have dealt with to do what. This requires an element of discipline. What do you do with business cards when you get them? Throw them away? Put them in a top pocket? Put them in a business card folder that's never looked at? Take the time to enter them into your network database. This is an area where it really does pay to be a squirrel. If you've got a great memory for people, that may be all you need. If, like me, you need a little more prodding, it's helpful to enter some summary text as well, particularly if you've a computer-based network database, so you can search for a particular topic.

Two final thoughts on the network database before we try an activity on your personal network. The first on the power of e-mail. We'll be going into electronic support in a lot more depth later, but the more your network database can include e-mail addresses the better. E-mail is the ideal way of giving your network a nudge. You can drop an e-mail to people with whom you have had only a fairly limited contact and ask them something you probably never would over the phone. It won't always get a response, but it is a brilliant way to reinforce relatively weak network links. The other is about the fourth dimension. Time is an important part of the tangled matrix that is your network. Be aware of the way time can hide things from you. Perhaps someone you last knew as a music student now owns a chain of restaurants. Over time some network links naturally weaken and others grow; time is always an influence.

The power of e-mail

A simple example of e-mail making the difference. I was writing an article on the office of the future. I had met a lecturer in computer sciences at a conference about a year previously. We had chatted over dinner, but that was all the contact we had; still, I had entered his business card into my network database. He was located in a university a couple of hundred miles away, so we were unlikely ever to bump into each other. When I was researching the article, I dropped him an e-mail. He referred me to a professor at a different university, again by e-mail, copying in the professor, so he knew I'd be in touch. I e-mailed the professor, who responded a few days later, agreeing to an interview. This chain of events simply wouldn't have happened before e-mail. There was no way I would phone someone on that limited acquaintance, while a letter would have involved much more cost and effort, and would be less likely to get a response.

Network mapping

Step 1   *Have your picture of your ideal activities, your goals and obstacles in front of you. Don't try to hold them in your head, this is something that really benefits from having it in black and white in front of your eyes.*

Step 2   *Explore your network. There's no point trying systematically to work through everyone; you'll never make it. Look through your address book and any business contact details you have. Envisage each individual, seeing if they have any relevance to your dream picture. If they do, jot them down. You might find it convenient to draw up a mind map with your goals and obstacles as branches, linking people to them as twigs.*

Going through an address book can be quite tedious. When you want a break, move on to Step 3.

Step 3   *Do a little random exploration. Let associations carry you around your network. Think of a key event. When you graduated. When you got your first car. The great storm of 1987. Whatever you use, think of the people who were close to you then. Your friends and business contacts. Have they any relevance? Do they make you think of anything else – spend five minutes bouncing your memories around.*

Step 4   *Return to the address book and repeat to taste. If you are a real glutton for punishment, try 'where are they now' on an old address book.*

Result *You won't have mapped your network (in this sense, the activity is misnamed), but you should have mapped part of your network on to your dream picture. You can now extract these people's names and go into some more detail, finding ways that you can use them (nicely, mutually, remember) to further your goals.*

Marketing yourself

Most of us are reasonably modest. We might not be shrinking violets, but it seems wrong to blow our own trumpets. What's more, we are suspicious of those who do seem to have excessive self-importance. Yet whichever approach you take to your portfolio, you will have to market yourself. In the new economy, when you are working *your* way, you are, in effect, selling yourself. That's your produce for the market. And there are few market stallholders who don't ensure that their produce looks its best.

This isn't about dressing right and cleaning your nails. Actually, that's a lie. There's no doubt at all that turning up inappropriately dressed will lower your chances of getting a job. That doesn't always mean wearing a suit, of course. I once turned up to interview the managing director of a medium-sized firm at his office. I agonized over what to wear. Should I match the corporate style and wear a suit, or dress down with my journalist look? I scrapped the tie, which was just as well, as my interviewee was wearing a sweatshirt.

Apple meets IBM

Famously, when IBM and Apple, two vastly different cultures, arranged a meeting over a joint venture, the IBM people, expected to be stiff-necked blue-suiters, turned up in T-shirts and jeans. The Apple employees, generally as scruffy as they come, dug out jackets and ties. It certainly broke the ice.

If your new activities are within your existing company, such marketing has to be fairly subtle. Is there some way to get your activity mentioned in an internal newspaper or bulletin?

Can you find someone who can drop a word in the right ear? Is there anything you can do for someone senior in your organization, or someone with a senior person's ear? The invention of the Post-it note within 3M, when a glue that didn't really work was found to be ideal for making markers in a choir member's hymnbook, is often related. What's relevant here, though, is not the invention but the internal marketing campaign that was used. The developer failed to sell the Post-it note to the 3M hierarchy. Undeterred, he had samples made and distributed them to senior executives' secretaries. By the time the supply ran out they were hooked – and clamouring for more. They were told they'd better persuade their bosses to develop the product. It happened.

If you are working externally, you can afford to be bolder. Make sure that you have the right material to look businesslike, even when you don't have a business. If you don't want the expense of business cards and a letterhead when you aren't even sure which way things are going, there are companies who supply blank fancy paper, or sheets of business cards, which you can run through a laser printer and produce very professional results (see the Chameleon Manager Web site for details). The important thing when marketing yourself is not to undersell. You might be modest, but there's no need to dig a pit for yourself. Be aware of your good points and be prepared to use them mercilessly. Always aim for a professional presentation. Your potential clients will want to do business with someone established, trustworthy and skilful. You'll have to busk the established bit by having confidence in yourself. The others, you should able to deliver.

Letterheads tip

If you need to have a letterhead printed at some point, consider whether you would benefit from having more than one style. Because of the way you work, or to have different levels of formality or simply for effect, you may like to have a range of letterheads. Thanks to Henry Berry of ideas consultancy Theory B for noticing that the paper used to produce letterheads is printed in a single block four times the size of the final sheet, which is then sliced up. There should only be a small difference in price between having four different letterheads (assuming the same colour combination) and having a single one.

The traditional work finder's kit

Your network is an indispensable means of locating work, but it isn't the only one. Conventional employment is often found through the job centre and the local paper. Neither of these are likely to be of much use to you, though it doesn't do any harm to scan the local paper (editorial, rather than advertising) to see what's going on as part of your survey of the world.

The national press and the trade press are more valuable. Whatever specialities you want to develop, there is probably some form of trade press. It's a great way of finding out what is happening. If you are having trouble locating a trade journal (many work by direct subscription), try the library (for information, rather than copies), ask your local chamber of commerce, or find someone already involved in the area and ask them. If you are looking for a direct job advertisement, either the specialist advertising in the national press or the trade press are probably your best bet, but when developing a portfolio, it may well be something in the editorial sections that catches your eye.

Electronic sources

Traditional sources haven't been overtaken by electronic yet, but there's no doubt that the Internet is making significant inroads. Chapters 6 and 7 will look in great detail at the power of information. Here we are concerned only with the opportunities for finding work. Jobs are advertised on the World Wide Web, on specific job location sites and on employers' sites. See the Chameleon Manager Web site for some examples. The advantage of searching the Web is that the speed and flexibility of the medium make it ideally suited to the more flexible jobs that are likely to fulfil a personal portfolio.

Even more importantly, though, the Web is rich with information about what companies and individuals are doing, and that is an ideal weapon in moving your aspirations towards reality. If you can find a company that is starting to do work in a field you can cover, or even companies who give the appearance of being the right sort of target, you have a better chance of success.

Trawling the Net

Step 1   *Get on to the World Wide Web. If you don't have access yet,*
bookmark this activity and come back to it when you do (when,
not if).

Step 2   *Take a keyword around one of the big goals in your portfolio. Use*
that keyword in a couple of Web search engines.

NOTE ...

Web addresses are notorious for becoming out of date, but at the time of
publishing two good search sites to try are http://www.altavista.digital.com and
http://www.yahoo.com.

Step 3   *Explore the results. Take a good half hour to do this. You aren't just*
looking for specific work opportunities, but also for interesting
information. Make a note of anything that seems relevant.

Result   *The outcome isn't predictable, that's one of the joys and frustrations*
of the Web. Sometimes you will be stunned by the amount of utterly
irrelevant rubbish there is (and the only likely looking response will
be in Norwegian). Sometimes you will come up with a treasure
trove of opportunities. Either way, you've gained a little more
experience with a key business tool.

Electronic selling

The information revolution provides a two-way channel. You
aren't only able to find out more about potential customers
by electronic means, they can find out about you too. You
can sell, for instance, using electronic mail, but be very
wary. E-mail is a very 'in your face' medium; it gets pushed
at you whether you like it or not. Unfortunately, because it's

so easy to send an e-mail to lots of people, it's a tempting way to sell a business proposition. This is great if the recipients are people you know – if the electronic network is overlaying your personal one. But it's the kiss of death to strangers. Unsolicited e-mail is even more of a curse than paper junk mail; don't use it. Oh, and one final thought on the e-mail front; if you intend to use mass mailing, make sure you've a mailing package that can hide all the other recipients from the message reader. Not only does it feel like a breach of confidence, there's nothing more infuriating than a three-line message preceded by a hundred lines of addresses.

Once again, though, it's the Web that dangles the biggest carrot. There's no doubt at all that a World Wide Web site is a great way to sell yourself or your products and services. We'll be looking at how to do this in the next section; for the moment, though, it's more a matter of being aware of just what you are doing. Setting up a Web site is like putting together a noticeboard. You can make it as attractive or dull as you like. You can put whatever information you like on it. Then you can put it in the public eye. The trouble is, you are dropping it into a field the size of Australia, with another 100 million notice boards. Then you wonder why you aren't getting much response.

If that was all there was to it, you might as well give up now. Yet thousands of businesses do very well, thank you. The secret is to get noticed. The Web is littered with search sites and indexes to help people find where they want to go. Make sure your site is listed. You can plod round submitting your site, or you can use one of the many automatic submission products. But search engines are just the start. Look round the newspapers (most have an on-line or hi-tech supplement) and magazines. See how other sites get a mention. Most computing magazines have a page with new, interesting sites on it. See if you can be included. Make sure your Web site is on all your ways of communicating with the world. In your e-mail signature, on your letterheads and business cards. And of course, use other sites. One of the principal ways people find a site is by a link from one they already know. Look for ways to get mentioned on other people's sites. Be imaginative. One of the activities in Chapter 5 will be to use a creativity technique to explore new ways of getting your site noticed; give it a try.

Practical commercial Web

The lowest level of commercial use for the World Wide Web is awareness. Letting potential customers know that you exist. Yet even if you use every technique we've discussed for getting your site noticed, there has to be some reason for the reader to stay there once they find it. It might be enough to say 'here I am' to have people beating a path to your door, but it helps to provide some sort of service that might be of use to the sort of people you want to attract.

As a simple example, I have a book section on my Web site (http://www.cul.co.uk/books), giving short reviews of titles which I recommend in general business, business creativity and science fiction. To make it more useful, if you see a book you'd like, or one you've heard about and haven't been able to find in the shops, there are links to on-line bookshops to enable the reader to pop straight over and buy a copy. This is tedious to set up, but it adds value to my site, making it more attractive for potential customers to come and have a look round. My business isn't selling books, it's consultancy – the book references are just a service to make my site more attractive.

There are plenty of other ways of doing something similar. You can provide information, like the Chameleon Manager Web site does. You can entertain, as many of the big commercial sites do. The main thing is that you make your site of value to the potential customer; you need a nice, big, juicy carrot to attract them in.

To most people, though, Internet commerce means selling through the Web. For a long time this was a non-starter. Various companies made high-profile ventures into selling on the Web, then quietly withdrew as it proved ineffective. In part, this early failure was down to lack of trust. The Internet was not a very safe medium by which to send a credit card number. Technically, that problem has now been resolved. If the right mechanisms are used, the Internet is very safe (certainly much more so than giving your credit card number over the phone). However, security was never the number one problem. This was offering an appropriate product range.

All too often a high street shop would offer a fraction of their usual product lines. Then they would be surprised if no one bought anything. The fact is, to work, a Web shop should offer at least as much and probably more than a conventional store. After all, you have to make the business of shopping this way more attractive than driving down to a local mall. One of the big advantages of electronic shopping is the ability to perform searches and match to your requirements – this is pointless if you only offer a small subset of your products.

Look for other benefits that can give an on-line shop the edge. If you live in a rural area you might have something to sell that is attractive to city dwellers that never pass your door. This market, often addressed through small advertisements in country magazines, covers a lot of the smaller shops on the Web, dealing in luxury or countrified items. Another way to make your site attractive is to give it some interactive benefit. For example, buying a computer or a car or insurance can be an intimidating process. There are so many options. A Web-based sales site can let you try out different possibilities and combinations, automatically calculating the cost as you change requirement. There's no salesperson breathing down your neck – you can do it at your own pace – and there's no obligation to buy, no embarrassment when you walk out without purchasing.

Setting up a Web commerce site is not an amateur business, but there are services to help which are well within the budget of a small or medium-sized company. If you feel you might want to start selling on the Web, see the Chameleon Manager site (http://www.cul.co.uk/chameleon) for some pointers to interesting shops.

Improbable tasks

A small but very important segment of your time in any portfolio is going to be spent putting in proposals. Whether you want to change the way your company sells sausages, or you have invented a new game, you need a proposal that clearly identifies what you want to do. Typically this would include the benefits for those who have to sanction it, what the costs are, who it is aimed at, and who you are – what makes you the ideal person to be involved. Of course proposals vary enormously. If your product is a story for a magazine, then the proposal amounts to little more than the story itself, a covering letter and return envelope. (Do remember the courtesies. Return postage may seem trivial to a big company and a lot to you, but you are much more likely to get a reply.)

This section is labelled improbable tasks because until you are a world-recognized expert in your field, most of your proposals will come to nothing. You will be rejected. This requires two responses. The first is a thick skin. No one likes rejection. No one likes to be told that their pet idea, which is clearly brilliant, stinks. I'll be honest, it doesn't get easier with practice. It still hurts. But as long as you eventually get some positive responses (it can take a long time), it is bearable. The second requirement is to keep up a constant flow of proposals out. The best counter to a rejection is to know that you have two other, even better proposals in the pipeline (or the same proposal to two, more enlightened, employers).

So your attempts to get tasks will often be improbable. Let's turn that round – you should also be applying for improbable tasks. Make sure that you are capable of delivering, but go for a whole range of possibilities. Make some proposals for something minor, others for meaty pieces of work. And some for a task that you know isn't going to go your way. Every now and then you may get a big, pleasant surprise. Of course it's highly unlikely, but one thing you know for certain is you'll never get it if you don't go for it.

Preparing for the tightrope

Expansion and moonlighting.
Using your network.
Failing and learning.
Using the Web to find and to promote.

Working *your* way involves building your own portfolio of activity. Much of it will be in a 'what if' state – not firm, but a possibility. Many of your early attempts will be failures. It's difficult. Western culture is not comfortable with failures in business. To go bankrupt is a stigma, while simply to make a wrong decision is a black mark for the future. This is something you will have to fight against. To be able to work your own way you will need to be able to make mistakes, learn from them and get started again quickly. As we saw in the previous section, rejections will happen – get back in there with two more. Technical faults will arise – try a couple of other directions to solve it.

The failures are worth persevering with, though, because through them we learn so much. Being able to fail fast requires a good mix of activities. It's part of what your portfolio is all about. Sometimes you'll get too much or too little – and that's where balance becomes so important. In the next chapter we will look at achieving that balance.

4 Balancing tasks – and life

 key concept | Managing more with less – turning stress into creative success.

Preview

- Juggling many balls.
- To some extent you can manage time, but you can't manufacture it.
- Balancing task searching, productive work and administration.
- You aren't alone - make use of your network.
- Stress is part of the equation.
- The time/cash/value/outcomes matrix.
- Don't wreck your home life.
- Working discipline.

One more ball in the air

It is almost inevitable that becoming a chameleon manager will mean having more different activities on the go at one time. It has been popular in management circles for a while to use juggling as a metaphor for the management role. Even if, like me, you find juggling itself physically challenging and about as exciting to watch as daytime television, the lessons are clear. It is possible to juggle more than you thought imaginable when you began, but you need to add balls one at a time, and each time you add a ball you will go back to failure until you master the technique.

This is where the gradual approach to a portfolio comes in handy. If you can take on a subsidiary activity first, then work it up to a significant part of a portfolio, then take steps to change your employment . . . and so on, you have a much better chance of keeping the balls in the air. This approach isn't always possible, of course. Sometimes, for example with redundancy, you are forced to change everything at once. Don't be tempted, though, to try to pick up your entire portfolio at once. Just because you are starting from scratch doesn't mean you've any better chance of succeeding with your full set of balls at once.

This chapter looks at ways of balancing your tasks, managing your time, using others to help and ensuring that work and home life are both part of the juggling act. As a result, you should find it a little easier to get another ball in the air, and to keep it there.

MORE INFO . . .

If the thought of juggling intrigues you (I can't think why), try *Juggling* by Lydia Darbyshire (Quintet, 1993).

The time management myth

A number of companies have done very nicely out of the whole business of time management. They have established the concept that to manage your time is to have your life under control. Certainly there is a negative truth here. Fail to manage your time, and the outcome will be chaos, especially in the hectic chameleon world. However it is also possible to become so tied up with the minutiae of time management that you don't give enough time to the job itself. Time management needs managing in its own right. If you have a box-ticking mind that loves to get everything just so, you can disappear into your time management folder for half the day by the time you've prepared your daily tasks and fed them back to your overall goals and integrated your essential schedule, and, and, and . . .

There's no doubt at all that a chameleon manager will need some time management, but it isn't necessary to rush out and buy yourself the entire system. A simple process, light on your time, should be enough. A task list and diary, coupled with a top ten concerns list should be enough for most people without resorting to complex forms and structures.

Time as master

Time is a strange thing. Although the passage of time can be objectively measured with incredible accuracy, subjective time is very variable. Take the time spent at work. For many conventional workers, the day can drag out interminably. The whole 'thank God it's Friday' culture depends on the fact that work is a bore, and at last you can let your hair down and enjoy yourself. On the other hand, a chameleon manager may well find there aren't enough hours in the day to get the job done, because it's so enjoyable. This is quite a bonus, but has to be treated carefully or the job can overwhelm your personal life, with disastrous consequences.

Whatever your attitude to time, it will occasionally be the master, whatever the gurus tell you. Don't take it too literally when they assure you that 'I'd love to, but I haven't the time' is an excuse. The argument is that you will make time if it is important enough. That's fine, but it doesn't allow for the fact that time manufacturing is a pretty tough art. In practice, mere mortals can't make time, we can only move it around. If something unexpected and totally dominant comes up and disrupts your schedule, however much you try to make time to catch up you will fail.

To an extent you can plan for time-as-master by building slack into your plans. If you are due to arrive at an important meeting requiring a one-hour drive down the motorway, you can leave an hour and a half before to cope with delays. To not do so would be very stupid. However, you can't sensibly allow for the very occasional time when you spend two hours stuck in a traffic jam; it would not be cost-effective. In such circumstances, you might as well recognize time is the master – otherwise you are going to hit problems with something covered later in the chapter: stress.

Time as servant

It's not all doom and gloom. As a chameleon manager you have some real advantages in the time control business. One aspect of time-as-master you can turn on its head is making use of your effective times. Everyone has times of day when they perform demanding or creative tasks best. Usually there are two or three peaks during the day. When you are controlling your portfolio you have a chance to make use of these times to maximize your quality and quantity of work – if you can't absolutely break the bonds of time, you can at least slacken them a bit by getting more out of the time available.

Time for a change

Simon is a computer programmer. For several years he worked for a large corporation. He was required to be at work by nine in the morning, and had to be out of the office by six in the evening. He was expected to turn up to work in a suit and tie. He was expected to polish his shoes and look respectable. By the end of his time with the company, Simon had settled into a rut of mediocrity. He was considered a very average programmer. He was frequently told off for turning up late, inappropriate standards of dress and dubious hairstyle. Both the company and Simon heaved a sigh of relief when the opportunity arose to take voluntary redundancy.

After six months without any work, Simon took on a contract job with a small software house. He was able to work from home or in the office. What he looked like and when he worked was of no real interest to the company, provided he delivered code on time. After a while he settled into a work style where he did no work at all in the mornings. He typically worked from mid-afternoon until early evening, then another stint from around midnight. Before long, Simon was the top-earning programmer and was taken on with a full-time contract. Interestingly, after a while, he took on a team leader role and modified his hours so that he had a greater overlap with his team (though he still spent little time in the office before midday). This was the same person, but exhibiting radically different performance, mostly down to him treating time as a servant.

As a chameleon manager you are also likely to have more control of your schedule than others. It is all too often true that a deadline is a whim or figment. You have a chance to challenge that and to make use of the flexibility of time to pack in other activities. Of course it's not all plain sailing. Those fixed deadlines you do have are liable to be more rigid than elsewhere because your performance will be measured against them, and you may not be used again if you fail to meet them. Even so, on the whole the chameleon manager is best placed to push time around a little.

The time graph

Most people are broadly aware of their best times of day, but they usually make scant use of them. In this activity you will plot your key time points. If you went through the perfect day activity in Chapter 2 you may like to keep that handy to act as a prompt.

Step 1   *Turn a sheet of paper sideways – lined paper is quite effective. List the hours of the day across the top.*

Step 2   *Draw a step graph through the day. Set three possible levels of energy: low, medium and high. Don't worry too much about exact timing, just get a broad feel. To give an idea of what's required, I have provided an example of my own graph.*

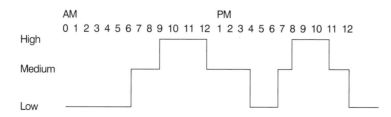

Step 3 *Put against each level the sort of activities that best suit a high, medium and low energy level for you. Examples might be:*

- ❍ *high – creative thought, new ideas, proposals, key meetings*
- ❍ *medium – other communication, everyday work, high-effort reading, other meetings*
- ❍ *low – low-effort reading, administration.*

Result *Put your chart somewhere obvious, so it can provide a reminder when you are booking activities in your diary (maybe you could laminate it and use it as a bookmark). Soon it will become habitual, but to begin with you will need a prompt. One way to force it into your diary is block off time for creative thought, for communication and for administration in the appropriate time sectors. Be prepared to argue when a key meeting is situated in a low-energy sector – the outcome will be disappointing for all concerned.*

A balanced diet

According to conventional wisdom, a worker in an old-style job spends all their time (apart from agreed lunch and coffee breaks) hard at work. This is nothing more than a convenient fiction. It is very entertaining when computing analysts have one of their regular bursts of doom-mongering about the Internet. 'Millions of workdays wasted browsing the Web' scream the headlines. It's tempting to wonder which planet these people live on. Do they really think that, were it not for Web access, these workdays would have been spent on productive work? Not a bit. Much more likely, they would have been spent discussing what was on television last night, the performance of a new car or the physical characteristics of the new window cleaner.

Think about your last working day. Did you have any non-productive time? What did you do? Could you really manage a working day without it?

In fact, most staff away from the production line, whatever the colour of their collar, spend a fair proportion of their working time detached from the job, interspersed with bursts of activity. When you begin to take more charge of your own time, such activities aren't going to stop, but you will be more aware of their impact. Time isn't money, but it could be. However, you will also have to be aware of extra activities that don't earn money but are essential. Even if you move to self-employment and get away from all the office politics and bureaucracy, you will still have to deal with your accounts and tax. In practice, with a decent accountant, the overhead isn't huge, but it exists and continues to make a call on your time. You will also find, as e-mail plays a larger part in your life (if it doesn't already) that it will take up to half an hour a day – any more, unless e-mail featured in your dream activities, and you need to re-examine your priorities.

A more significant non-earning drain is liable to be the time spent finding work and laying the ground for possible future work. Apart from the obvious need to ensure that this doesn't so eat into earnings that you aren't solvent, there is a more subtle balance to be achieved. Future work is generally probabilistic. Some potential work will be a long shot, others very likely. Don't be tempted to ignore the long shots. It's usual for anyone's dream portfolio to contain one or more areas that involve unlikely odds. The ideal combination is a long shot which involves very little effort before the sale. If the long shot is going to involve a lot of work it will have to be a background, hobby-style task. Provided there is no more than half an hour of preparation, long shots should be a regular part of your working diet. A practical approach is to have a weekly long shot task – make one low-probability, low-effort application a week.

Balancing probabilities

Bill is a salesman who is developing his hobby of model-making to broaden his portfolio. He has contacts in two model shops who will buy high-detail model railway trucks made from kits to sell on to railway enthusiasts who can't be bothered to make them themselves. Such tasks are high effort, low risk – he has to put the effort in up front, but he knows that he is likely to make a sale and there are many possible buyers. When Bill sees that a new business is opening, he contacts them to see if they would be interested in a purpose-built model for their shop or reception. Bill only sends out an introductory sheet with photographs of models he has made before. This is low effort but high risk. Bill is unlikely to get a response, but when he does it is very lucrative (and enjoyable). In his spare time, Bill is working on a model of the first car made by a particular manufacturer. When it is finished, he will enquire to see if the manufacturer would be interested in buying it. This is a high effort and a very high risk as there is only one possible buyer and they might not be interested. However, for Bill, the possibility of getting his model into the company's headquarters, and the enjoyment of making this model is enough to keep him going. The status means, though, that it will remain a spare-time activity.

Bringing in the network

We've already looked at the network as a source of work. It's easy to forget that it is also a resource to help with balance. In Chapter 12 we will be looking at the concept of a mentor, a member of your network to use as a sounding board for your business ideas and propositions. A mentor can help you to get a clearer view of your priorities and can assist with steering a course between tasks and life. But that's not all your network can do to help. In fact, you can use your network to get rid of work.

At first sight the thought of giving up work is worrying. Self-employed chameleon managers can be particularly nervous of turning down any offer of work, while to the employed it sounds like the sort of action that doesn't exactly lead to a positive performance review. To take this view overlooks the contribution of the network. There's a need to have a more creative outlook. In direct employment what you are doing is delegating, not shirking. If working for yourself, you are ensuring that you continue to have a record of delivering what the customer wants, even though in practice someone else will be doing the work and collecting the reward.

Most of all, though, you will be establishing the grounds for reciprocal support. If you are in consultancy (or plumbing or whatever) and you pass some work on to a fellow consultant, you can reasonably expect some return consideration in similar circumstances. If you realize that you have taken too much work on, don't drive yourself into the ground, bring someone in. How you approach this depends on the circumstances. If you provide mutual support for another chameleon manager this might be done as explicit subcontracting or by making your lifeline a nameless part of your team. Perhaps the most satisfactory approach if you are likely to make regular use of an individual is to advertise him or her as part of your assets – and be prepared to reciprocate. That way you appear to have more talent on board than you actually have. (Remember that the chameleon is good at deception. But don't worry, this is positive deception because you aren't being misleading. The talent really is on board, you just don't own it.)

Stressing out

Stress is a difficult problem. Taken to excess it can be a killer, yet without any pressure or deadline most activities lack bite. In fact, the more you move to a self-managed portfolio, the more chance you have of managing stress. Often you will be escaping entirely some of the typical stressors – the same, increasingly congested journey to work every day, the office politics, the fight for budgets and survival. Against this you will have to add the stresses inherent in having no long-term certainty and managing your own time more, but as we've already established long-term certainty is an illusion however you work.

Whichever stage you are at in developing your portfolio, there will be times when it is necessary to reduce stress. Try to incorporate as many de-stressing components as you can into your work environment. This is particularly easy if you manage your own portfolio and work in your own office. Play music (or have silence) while you work. Surround yourself with items you like. Put as much effort into choosing your work chair as you would the furniture in your sitting room – chances are you spend at least as much time in it.

Most people also have favoured activities they find reduce stress. Whether it's eating sweets, jogging or shooting spaceships in a game, make sure that you can access a de-stressing activity when you need to, and don't be ashamed to engage in it during your working day, as long as it remains a brief activity and doesn't take over. When hit by sudden stressors, like an aggressive phone call, simple breathing exercises can be handy to relieve stress.

Rather less frequently there is a need to increase stress. When giving a series of creativity courses with a co-presenter recently, we had an afternoon session where two of the attendees said that we seemed to lack interest in what we were doing. This wasn't the case, but repetition, a hot room and lack of sleep had combined to give an uninspiring performance. For the next afternoon session we consciously hyped ourselves up, with significantly better results. Don't think, by the way, that because you don't do training or theatre that you don't perform. Any business presentation, any communication is a performance where you need energy if you are going to put your message across convincingly. And stressing up can be equally valuable when working on your own at a desk. How often have you been an hour into writing (or even worse, reading) a report and felt washed out?

Stressing yourself up is easier than removing stress, especially as you only need apply positive stress. Go outside, especially if it's a cold day. Move around violently. Jump, punch the air, yell (if you can do so without embarrassment – that's the wrong sort of stress). If there's someone else to help, you can play off each other. Get very silly – quote a Monty Python script or whatever current humorous topic has taken your fancy. Engage in anything that gets colour into your cheeks, makes your eyes feel wide open and brings a smile to your lips.

Stressing out

As a potential killer, stress is important, yet this is probably the activity that you are most likely to skip over. Resist the urge. You need to control your stress levels.

Step 1   *Think back through the last week. What has caused you stress? Note down the incidents, however minor. If you happen to have had the one stress free week of the year, go back to another week. You* *should be able to accumulate a good number. Getting stuck behind that slow lorry on a long winding road, the child who wouldn't stop crying, the committee that refused to pay heed to your recommendation, the meeting with the chief executive.*

Step 2   *Think a little bit about each example of stress. What caused it? Why was that incident stressful? It might have been life threatening, embarrassing, or just plain irritating. Why? Try to dig as deep as you can.*

Step 3   *For each of the stress causes you have identified, try to come up with an antidote. It might involve putting the problem into perspective, revenge (imagined or real), distraction, breathing or physical exercise, simple acceptance that the situation is entirely out of your hands, or another route. This is so personal that there is very little guidance than can be given – the fact is, though, in the calm view of distance you may well be able to see an antidote that wasn't available to you on the spot.*

Acceptance

A classic application of acceptance is when stuck in a traffic jam. For years I was really stressed up when I knew that, as a result of getting stuck I was going to be late for a meeting. I now find, provided I've done everything possible (a mobile phone helps, to call and explain), I can sit back and relax say 'it's entirely out of my hands. I'm late now – there's nothing I can do about it'. The better your in-car entertainment, the more effective this ploy.

Result   *As a result of this exercise you should have a number of personal antidotes to stress – a stress first aid kit. When you feel stress coming on, try mentally to pull out the kit and apply an antidote. It will take practice to get this to work. You won't have all the right antidotes – you need to build your kit over time – and you won't have enough self-control always to apply them. Yet with time you will be able to manage your stress more effectively, and you owe that to yourself.*

What's it worth?

Any chameleon manager is liable to face the challenge of performing different tasks with different cash values. Traditionally professionals have been rated financially on their input. Salaries are decided not on what individuals actually produce, but on the nature of the job and the context. So we see nurses arguing for parity with teachers, or clinical psychologists with doctors. You, however, will have a more complex task. You have to rate the value of your output against the market. This becomes particularly challenging with a parallel work portfolio. Each different task may carry a different pay rate.

The knee-jerk reaction is only to do the best-paid work. Unfortunately, this laudably simple proposition is likely to be incompatible with your goals. If you were only in it for the money, this could be a winning strategy, but most people who have tested their dream employment go for a mix of cash, personal fulfilment and more. There are also strategic and tactical considerations. Do you go for the steady mid-priced job, or undertake a low-paid activity which has a chance of generating a high return in the future? What's more, the supply of tasks does not always follow your personal inclination. Even if you did choose to go only for the high-paid work, you cannot guarantee a constant source of work over time.

A man who knows the price of everything and the value of nothing. (Oscar Wilde defining a cynic in *Lady Windermere's Fan*)

The reason this balance is so difficult is that you are working in four dimensions at once. If this sounds impossibly challenging, bear in mind that this is exactly what a three-year-old is managing to do when walking along the street, negotiating the three spatial dimensions and a fourth of time by the indirect mechanism of speed. When balancing tasks, the three dimensions which are added to time are money, thrill and onward business.

What can be particular surprising to those still in conventional employment is the variation in payment a chameleon manager might accept. The extremes of my activities are writing books and creativity consultancy. If you only consider the advance paid when the book is written, the factor between writing and consultancy can easily be sixty to one. Let me write that again slowly. Sixty times as much money for the same amount of effort. Even though I am used to such bizarre ratios, it is hard to believe that a sane person would conceive of parallel working on such wildly different levels of return. But remember that money is only one input.

Examined outside the field of finance, writing a book has a lot going for it. It is high on the thrill dimension. There is something uniquely satisfying about having a book on the shelf with your name on the spine. In my case, writing is something I actually enjoy doing, so I have a doubly valued activity. Then there's the onward business aspect. This is a tough one if you are uncomfortable with probability, because onward business is predicted, not certain. Some jobs are one-offs, unconnected to anything else that might happen. But others have a network of new business possibilities extending out from them. If I write a book, it might become a best-seller and make me rich. It might have a film based on it (okay, pretty unlikely for a business book, but you never know). It might lead to other book contracts. And it can prove the basis for consultancy, acting as a credential with clients.

I don't have a magic formula for this decision. The important thing is to ensure that you are making the choices consciously rather than implicitly. In this process you should be ensuring that you are earning as much money as you need to, but also making sure that you have some thrills targeted, and that some of the activities you undertake have onward business potential that could bring in more work in the future.

The value balance sheet

It is informative to see how your personal portfolio, however uncertain at this stage, comes out on the various dimensions.

Step 1   *List your dream activities from Chapter 2. After them put four columns headed: 'Money', 'Thrill', 'Onward business' and 'Availability'.*

Step 2   *Leaving the fourth column for the moment, assess each activity in the first three. You can do this on a fairly broad basis – high, medium or low, but it is better if you can work to more detail. Rate them out of ten, or give them a rough amount per hour (monetary).*

Step 3   *Complete the 'Availability' column. Entries should range on a scale from one-off to continuous.*

Result   *In practice, you are likely to decide whether to take on tasks based on a combination of gut feel (for thrill and onward business) and simple economics. However, having a picture of your ratings might help you deal with conflict.*

Keeping home safe

Bringing work home is generally a disaster. The work doesn't get done properly and your home life is disrupted. When I had staff working for me, I tried to make sure as much as possible that they didn't take work home. And I tried to set an example myself. If I really needed to work at the weekend, I would go into the office. This has two effects. It avoids spoiling the time you actually are at home, and it concentrates the mind wonderfully. In fact, I would go as far as to say that if you do work in an office you ought to go in half a day a month at the weekend just for the experience. There's a strange illicit thrill to being there when you shouldn't be, especially if you make things different by going in casual clothes, taking a pizza and playing music as you work.

There is a danger that goes with taking on your own portfolio. However you accomplish it, you are liable to have more mingling of work and home. This has its good points. After all, for many people part of the dream is to spend more time with their family. A senior director of a large British firm, discussing the pressures of business, commented that he had missed out on the entire upbringing of his children. Apart from infrequent holidays and occasional weekends he would leave for work before the children were out of bed and come home when they were asleep. 'But,' he commented, 'this is the price you have to pay if you want to get on in business.' He was making a huge and invalid assumption; the chameleon manager shouldn't be prepared to accept such a compromise. The reward isn't worth the price, especially as it is possible to manage both. So moving to your own managed portfolio will give you the chance to spend more time with your family/pets/car/friends/lover (delete where applicable).

What's the catch, then? It becomes harder to make that clear distinction between work and domestic life that was under threat when work was brought home. Especially if you work from home, the dividing line is very fine. To avoid disaster it is necessary to have clear distinctions, accepted by everyone. A separate room helps in this, as does agreed working times. Of course this goes against the ideas of freedom that being a chameleon manager should imply, but for those who don't live alone, it is necessary to balance family life as part of your dream portfolio.

'I could never be so disciplined'

The most frequent reaction I get when I describe how I work is 'I could never be so disciplined'. It seems that most of us looking at self-management from the safety of a regular job feel that we would go to pieces without constant monitoring. Perhaps the basis for this feeling is the ease with which we can be distracted when we bring work home for the weekend. To begin with, there may be similar environmental problems for those who move to a self-managed portfolio. There is inevitably going to be a transitional phase, and depending on the distractions in your new working environment it may prove uncomfortable for a while.

If you are working from home, a separate room from the other daytime occupants of the house is essential. This needn't be a dedicated room – in fact it is probably best for you if it isn't, as use of a dedicated room may necessitate payment of business rates – but you do need a mechanism for shutting out any distractions and noise that might be in the house. Contrary to expectation, children may be less of a problem with interruptions than partners are. Children quickly learn that a room is out of bounds, but your partner is liable to see you around and try to borrow you for various domestic requirements. In a crisis this is obviously advantageous, and having more time for domestic matters might have been part of the reason for adopting this working style, but you do need to establish an explicit contract with your partner about what is acceptable, and your need to have time to work.

MORE INFO . . .

A good start to identifying some of the business implications of working for yourself or from home is the *Lloyds Bank Small Business Guide* by Sara Williams (Penguin, annual). You are also likely to need an accountant – not a pleasant thought for some people, but most of them are house trained.

Even if you aren't working from home, there is liable to be more need for self-discipline than with a traditional job. You need to balance your tasks and life in a way that pleases a wider range of stakeholders than you would normally expect. It is possible that some people will find this very difficult. The fact remains, though, that this is the business environment an increasing percentage of us will be working in, and the solution is not to bemoan your own lack of discipline, but to look at ways to improve it. A combination of performing tasks that you really want to do and the need to keep money flowing in is usually an effective persuader.

Balancing into creativity

 key concept
Have a balanced diet.
Use your key times.
Manage stress.
Be prepared to have a wide range of tariffs.
Keep your home life safe.

With well-managed time, a good balance between productive and non-productive work, an understanding of how you can deal with undertaking different activities with wildly varying rates of remuneration and a fair share between home and work, you should be able to manage the juggling act that is part of being a chameleon manager. It is never going to be trivial. The very nature of the beast is change and adaptability. Yet keeping a balance is not only possible but, like juggling, is significantly easier than it looks.

On its own, though, the ability to balance your tasks isn't enough. The challenges we face in business are increasingly tough, and the chameleon manager is more likely to have to deal directly with some of the implications of change than a conventional employee. This requirement is not without benefit. In exchange for showing such flexibility, the chameleon manager has a more interesting, exciting, rewarding, fulfilling (you get the picture) time of it. But there is a need to deliver creativity and innovation with challenging regularity. Without creative skills, the chameleon manager has little chance of achieving her or his goals.

5 The creative urge

| key concept | Managing live innovation. |

Preview

- Every chameleon manager needs creativity.
- There are well-established techniques which can enhance personal and group creativity.
- Imagination Engineering – applying creativity in a four-stage process.
- Using creativity to improve your portfolio.
- Managing innovation in the workplace.

What's it for?

Imagination, which, in truth, is but another name for absolute power. (William Wordsworth in *The Prelude*)

Creativity is a strange concept. We are more used to it as an input to the arts than a requirement in business. Yet solving a business problem or coming up with an idea for a new product or service is just as innovative as writing a play or painting a picture. Looking from the artistic viewpoint, there's a certain reluctance to explain what creativity is *for*. Many artists would argue that art stands alone, without any need for value or utility. It's arguable, though, that this attitude is why we have moved away from art that is appreciated by the public, to art that can only be appreciated by academics. Form has become more important than function; much modern art doesn't give, it takes.

In business, creativity has to be something different from this. Business creativity is worthless unless it makes something happen, unless it achieves a goal. If the business problems we faced (classing the search for a new product or idea as a type of problem) were easily resolvable by reference to past experience, they wouldn't exist. There wouldn't be a problem because you could pull out a cookbook, follow the directions and fix it. Real life isn't like that. Finding effective solutions can only be achieved by looking at the problem, or the solution, in a different way. Business creativity is all about solving problems in a new way, one which breaks out of the conventional approach and introduces something unusual, something out of the ordinary.

Mechanical creativity

In itself, this description of the need for creativity can be quite frustrating. It's all very well for highly creative people, but what about the rest of us? Does it mean we should all be looking for someone very creative to solve our problems? It certainly wouldn't do any harm to get some creative people involved, as a very direct way of looking at a problem in a different way can be to get someone else's view. Yet it isn't enough. You, yourself, have to be creative.

It doesn't help that the conventional picture of creativity is sitting in the bath, or under an apple tree and suddenly being struck by inspiration (or an apple). This isn't a very satisfactory way of using creativity in business. You might have to wait an awfully long time for the inspiration to strike, and even when it does, a competitor will probably have thought of half a dozen better approaches first. What's needed is a mechanical way of being creative. A method that is as simple, practical and reliable as a mechanical tool.

At first sight this is an unlikely requirement. After all, creativity is the very antithesis of mechanicalism. It's what separates us from machines. However clever a computer may be at playing chess, it is only following rules. Before computers can be creative they will have to be capable of inventing a game like chess in the first place. Luckily, though, from the early days of the wheel and the lever, humanity has proved ingenious at using things mechanical to aid our internal capabilities. Just as a lever increases the lifting capabilities of the hands that push on it, there are creativity techniques which magnify anyone's ability to be creative.

Techniques in action

The theory behind a creativity technique is simple. We are all trapped in a conventional mode of thought. Experience, society and education have all taught us that certain things work, certain things are acceptable and others just don't fit. Creativity techniques temporarily suspend the rules and push our thoughts out of their habitual path. They provide a stimulation to look at the problem in a different way. There is nothing magical about this, but the effect can be astounding.

MORE INFO . . .

Serious Creativity by Edward de Bono (HarperCollins, 1993) and *A Whack on the Side of the Head* by Roger von Oech (Warner, 1983) are good guidebooks to general creativity techniques. It is often hard to find creativity guides in bookshops. Check http://www.cul.co.uk/books.

Since the 1940s a number of workers have been developing creativity techniques, but all of them rely to some extent on this same approach. There isn't room here to provide a full guide to creativity – there are plenty of other books doing that – but I can give you an introduction to a particular approach and describe a few of the techniques which can help make business creativity a reality.

Imagination Engineering

One of the problems you face when trying to become more creative is working out how to apply what can seem like a chaotic mess of techniques. The very existence of a book by James M. Higgins entitled *101 Creative Problem Solving Techniques* (New Management Publishing, 1994), emphasizes the range of options available. To help make creativity practical, a popular approach is the Imagination Engineering framework. The book of the same name gives much more detail, but in essence the framework breaks down creative problem-solving into four stages.

MORE INFO . . .

For a full and entertaining exposition of business creativity, see *Imagination Engineering* by Paul Birch and Brian Clegg (Pitman Publishing, 1996).

Stage 1: surveying the problem area

The first stage of Imagination Engineering is to survey the problem area. This activity falls into two broad categories. One is about building a picture of the information surrounding your problem. The other is looking for different ways of describing a problem. It is not uncommon to be unsure exactly what the problem is, so at this early stage it is worth putting some effort into clarifying your requirement.

A good way of building up your survey of the environment of your problem is to use a mind map (see Chapter 2, page 17 for more details of mind maps). Sketch out what you know already. To help fill out some detail, ask what will happen if you take no action whatsoever. In some cases this may be not only a part of the survey, but also the solution. It is not unheard of to find that there are no real disadvantages to the cheap and cheerful option of doing nothing. More often, though, there will be consequences. Use these consequences to establish a clearer picture of your problem area.

There are a number of creativity techniques to refine your idea of what the problem is. A very simple one is repeatedly asking the question 'Why?'. Say your problem was 'how to increase productivity by 10 per cent'. The reply to 'Why?' might be 'Because we need to improve profitability before the year end'. Again ask 'Why?'. 'To impress a potential investor.' 'Why?' 'Because we want to expand into the Pacific.' And so on. Each of these answers gives a possible new slant on the problem. Instead of saying 'how to increase productivity' we might say 'how to impress a potential investor' or 'how to expand into the Pacific'. This technique helps to overcome the assumptions you have been making (for example, that we need a new investor if we are going to expand into the Pacific), allowing for alternative possibilities.

Another, equally simple approach is the obstacle map we used in Chapter 2 (see page 24 to establish what was getting in the way of our dream portfolio. Each of the obstacles in a problem-solving session can be considered a new 'how to' in their own right – how to remove the obstacle.

The level chain

In this activity we are going to use another creativity technique that helps establish direction – the level chain. The level chain is particularly good for developing new product concepts. It fits in with the first stage, surveying the problem area, because to begin with you don't know in which direction you are going, but it often also encompasses the second stage, generating ideas.

Step 1   *The level chain starts with an existing product or concept. Choose something associated with the area in which you are trying to come up with a new idea. If you have nothing in mind right now, try to come up with a new financial service, starting from a piggy bank.*

Step 2   *From your starting point, generate a chain of other products or concepts. Each can be higher or lower in level than the previous one it is linked to – it doesn't matter which. So, for instance, if we were starting from a sausage, we might go up in level to a cylinder* or to a meat product, or we might go down in level to a pork sausage or a Cumberland sausage. To make it clearer, I have illutrated two chains from piggy bank.

In this chain we first go up to a more general form, a pig. Then down to a specific breed of pig, then down again, intentionally misinterpreting the previous entry to a specific sort of spot – a spot prize. Now an idea strikes. How about a form of savings account with lower than usual interest, but regular cash prizes, like a lottery? You could combine saving and gambling. Let's try again in another illustration.

Here we went up again, but this time to a money box. Further up to a container, then down to a specific container – a hamburger container. Here another idea struck. Why not have mini-banks in hamburger restaurants? The youth market is key to banks gaining new customers: this way you could make banks less threatening places and get teenagers used to banking services in an environment which they are very comfortable with.

Step 3

Whenever you hit on an idea, or something that makes you think of an idea, stop. There is no right place to stop – just when something strikes. The important thing with the level chain is that it is a quick technique. Don't analyse what you are doing, just run along a chain without really thinking. You should be able to do several in a couple of minutes.

Result

Out of a very quick exercise you could have generated some impressive new possibilities. The level chain is a good example of the creativity technique in action – in a whole afternoon of

*discussion and brainstorming you might not have come up with a
savings account with low interest and prizes, or banks in
hamburger restaurants. Keep the level chain in mind whenever you
need a new product or service, whether it is to expand your
personal portfolio or to help the company you work for.*

Stage 2: building ideas – the random picture

With the problem clarified, we reach Stage 2. The power
creativity techniques are brought into play to generate a range
of new ideas. There are many possibilities here; we will look
at two.

The random picture technique starts (unsurprisingly) with a
randomly selected picture. The word 'random' is important. If
you try to fit the picture to the problem, you are missing the
whole point. Remember that creativity techniques are about
forcing you out of your habitual approach. The sheer
randomness of the picture will help this to happen. For a
quick random picture, you could pick up any Sunday
supplement and choose the first picture. If you are going to
use this technique more regularly, it would be worth investing
in one of the many thick books of colour photographs you can
find in any remaindered bookshop at very reasonable prices.
Make sure it's a general photography book, or one that covers
a wide range of subjects (e.g. one with stills from different
types of film). Generally you can get away with finding a
random picture by letting the book fall open, but if this
doesn't work for you, you can use a spreadsheet to generate
a list of random numbers between 1 and the number of pages
in the book, and select using these.

Once you have your random picture, put your problem aside
for a moment. Don't think about the problem, think about the
picture. What does it remind you of? What can you see in it,
looking at both the whole and individual elements? What
associations does it have for you? Having established the
answer, link some of the elements and associations back to
your problem. It's surprising how often a randomly selected

THE CREATIVE URGE

picture will enable you to come up with a huge array of relevant possibilities. Note 'possibilities'. You are not attempting perfect solutions at this stage, just wild and wonderful ideas which you will later refine.

Something like the random picture technique is best illustrated by example. Say we were looking for a way of improving staff morale. I pick a random picture from my book. It shows a misty country scene. In the foreground is the back wheel of an old wooden cart. The cart stands in lush grass with clover and wildflowers. In the middle distance a neat, white painted chapel is surrounded by a picket fence. It has a belfry, but no bell. This makes me think of barn dances, going to church in Sunday best, Tom Sawyer painting the fence, the Irish countryside, the Hunchback of Notre Dame, Jersey cows and much more. Just from those associations, some ideas to help with my problem start to pop up. Hold a social event, a barn dance perhaps. Pay for smart clothes for customer contact staff. Tom Sawyer got other people to paint the fence for him – have a 'do someone else's job day'. Jersey cows – take them all out for a cream tea. And so on.

Leonardo at work

Although the explicit use of creativity techniques only dates back to the 1940s, Leonardo da Vinci came up with some of his remarkable inventions by using a variant of random picture. He would doodle on a piece of paper with his eyes closed, then look at the picture and see what it inspired in him. The doodle was used exactly the same way as is a modern creativity technique, to move him away from his conventional line of thought.

Getting your site noticed

In Chapter 3 we noted the difficulty of getting a site on the World Wide Web noticed. In this activity you are going to use a creativity technique both to find out a bit more about creativity, and to improve the chances of your Web site succeeding.

The technique you are going to use is 'random word'. This is very similar to the random picture technique just described, but uses a word for stimulus rather than a picture. Remember that the randomness is important. When you first get a word you might be tempted to pick a new one, because the word chosen isn't relevant. Don't give in to the temptation. Stick with it.

Step 1   On a blank sheet of paper, note down the problem – getting your Web site noted. Then spend a minute jotting down the obvious solutions. We are looking for creative solutions, so it's handy to put the obvious to one side while you come up with something more spectacular.

Step 2   Now you are going to take a significant step away from the problem. To push yourself into a different viewpoint you need a stimulation. I have listed sixty words. Pick one at random by glancing at the second hand of a watch and noting exactly which second is pointed at. Take that number from the list.

1. Cactus	21. Train	41. Holly bush
2. Glider	22. Cake	42. Space shuttle
3. Moon	23. Milk	43. Slaughterhouse
4. Airport	24. Beach	44. Champagne
5. Christmas	25. Supermarket	45. Massage
6. Submarine	26. Filing cabinet	46. Cathedral
7. Bed	27. Traffic light	47. Cheetah
8. Dentist	28. Lawyer	48. Parachute
9. Party	29. Wine	49. Gun
10. Swing	30. Matches	50. Elephant
11. Road	31. Magic	51. Circus
12. Artist	32. Song	52. Map
13. North Pole	33. Shipwreck	53. Potter
14. Pyramid	34. Tree	54. Vampire
15. Snowman	35. Leaf	55. Bud
16. Roof	36. Stone circle	56. Library
17. X-ray	37. Olympics	57. Old movies
18. Joystick	38. Scissors	58. Night-dress
19. Brick	39. Thong	59. Barbecue
20. Arrow	40. Plastic	60. Dolphin

THE CREATIVE URGE

Step 3   *On a separate piece of paper, note down the associations the word has for you. What does it make you think of? What real, literary, historical, personal associations has it? Keep your notes to short, two-word statements. Spend a couple of minutes on this.*

Step 4   *Now return to your problem. How could the associations you have written down influence your thinking on getting a Web site used more? What aspects of the problem do the associations make you think of? Be as wild as you like: don't try to be practical.*

Step 5   *Technically that's all we need to do at the building stage of creativity. You have generated ideas. However, it is worth taking a few – the most appealing, however impractical – and spending a minute or two to consider how you could change them to make them practical without killing the appeal. For example, if you had decided you could make your Web site more attractive by giving everyone who used it £1 million, you are likely to get a very popular site, and a very sudden bankruptcy. However you could look at ways to modify the idea by still giving something away, but making it more realistic and, ideally, more likely to generate trade.*

Result   *From this process you should obtain a number of ideas. Don't worry if they are ill-formed or even if you don't get much of a result. Using creativity techniques is hugely dependent on practice. The more you try these techniques, the easier they will become.*

True randomness

When using the random word technique, there is in fact a degree of cheating. The words in the list above are chosen to be reasonably concrete and to have associations which are likely to generate ideas. It is perfectly acceptable to use a more general and truly random method of choosing words. I have used a dictionary (selecting a page number, then entry number), a magazine and an electronic dictionary to achieve the same result. The electronic dictionary is particularly entertaining, as you can enter a nonsense word into either a word processor spell-checker or a hand-held electronic dictionary and have it produce a word at random. In such circumstances, however, you do have to be prepared to reselect if the word is unsuitable. In a recent exercise, the word generated was 'notwithstanding'. It was generally felt that this lacked associations. However, if you are taking this approach, you need to avoid dropping words just because they don't feel appropriate to the problem. Only omit them if they are incapable of generating associations.

Building ideas: someone else's view

Another technique that's easy to pick up is 'someone else's view'. One of the best sources of creativity is a small child. They are yet to have been indoctrinated with what is and isn't possible or 'right', and so they offer some very original thinking. The Polaroid camera was devised as a result of a child's disappointment that photographs which had just been taken couldn't be seen immediately. Unfortunately, children are rarely available from office suppliers, so you will need to take a slightly different approach.

In this technique you think yourself into the persona of someone in history, a fictional character or a particular type of person. What would Winston Churchill, Rambo or a plastic surgeon make of your problem? How would they solve it? What new insights can you gain from their thoughts? Don't worry if the linkage of the person and the problem is totally anachronistic. Genghis Khan, for example, might not know what a trade union was, but he'd certainly have some interesting thoughts on placating them. As before, don't try to match the person to the problem. The best approach is to put together a list of interesting people and fictional characters (don't make the mistake of making them all likeable) and choose one at random. If you are having a group problem-solving session, each member of the group could take on a character. If the context is appropriate they may even role-play the character.

The dating game

This creativity technique was especially devised for The Chameleon Manager. *It is a variation on 'someone else's view'. To use it you will need a dictionary of dates – the lists of events that happened on a particular date. You will find such lists in encyclopaedias (including the electronic variety) and various other sources of reference. I used* A Dictionary of Dates *by Cyril Leslie Beeching (Oxford University Press, 1993).*

Step 1   *Select a problem to solve – it can be personal or business related. Look up today's date. Pick out two or three entries which appeal because they are bizarre, exciting or otherwise stimulating. As I write this it is 7 January. On this day in 1558 the French took Calais from the British, one of the Montgolfier brothers (the first successful balloonists) was born, as was the French composer, Francis Poulenc.*

Step 2   *Now take each event or person. Imagine yourself at the event, or being that person. How would you look at the problem? What would you do about it? What different perspectives would you get from the event or from the sort of activity this person undertook? Would your period in history lead to any interesting misunderstandings? Jot down your thoughts.*

Step 3   *Combine the thoughts and perspectives from the different viewpoints. Some will be immediate ideas that only need refining. Others will be a starting point for generating ideas – impractical in itself, but full of inspiration. For instance, if I was trying to work out how to get late payers to respond to my invoices, Montgolfier might consider dropping leaflets on his debtors from his balloon, Poulenc might play horrendous music until they pay up (don't get me wrong – I love Poulenc's music, the idea of producing music is the starting point) and Calais makes me think of seizing the money by force. Refinements on these ideas might be a solicitor's letter, repeated irritating phone calls and sending in the bailiffs respectively.*

Result   *The dating game is a useful variant on 'someone else's view'. The latter works best when you have plenty of time and the participants can really get themselves into character, perhaps even dressing up for the part. The dating game can be used in a more quick and free way as the stimulation is broader, and has the added fun of the 'on this day' input to inject freshness into a creativity session.*

What about all the other ideas?

Many people have a real concern when they start using creativity techniques. The sheer randomness is going to mean that you only come up with a certain subset of all the possible solutions to your problem. What if you've missed the best one? What about all the other ideas you have not come up with?

In fact, this is a rather illogical reaction. After all, simply waiting for inspiration isn't going to come up with all possible ideas either. It is liable to come up with far fewer. When using creativity techniques you have to be entirely pragmatic. If you've got a good answer that does the job, what does it matter if there is a better one somewhere? Practically any problem will have a range of solutions. Your task is not to find every solution, nor even to find the best. It is to find a workable solution which does all that is required of it (this may include being better than everyone else's solution; that doesn't make it the best, only the best so far known). Once you've reached that solution, looking for anything else is a waste of time.

Stage 3: transforming ideas

The building process will throw out lots of ideas. Some mundane and obvious, others wild and wacky. At the third stage of Imagination Engineering you need to transform these ideas into workable propositions. First weed mercilessly. Don't throw out ideas because they're unworkable - practicality comes later. Instead discard anything that is obvious, doesn't excite you, seems mundane. Leave yourself with a

THE CREATIVE URGE

few, really outstanding, appealing ideas. Now spend two minutes examining just the good points of the ideas. Squash any negative thoughts or comments as soon as they arise. Note only the good. After that spend a similar time on bad points. When you have the key bad points listed, consider how you are going to do something about them. For a quick problem-solving session this would merely involve top-of-the-head actions. If you are taking several days to address a major problem you will probably take these bad points as problems to use building techniques against in their own right. At the end of this process you should have at least one original, remarkable, yet workable solution.

The demon practicality

When you first begin to use creativity techniques you will have a real fight with yourself (and anyone else involved) to suppress practicality. You will automatically try to weed out 'silly' ideas as you think of them. Leave them in. When you come to transform the output of building you will want to keep only the practical ideas. Resist. Be particularly careful in a group session if someone is writing down the ideas immediately they are voiced that they don't censor the ideas they think are impractical by ignoring them.

Stage 4: making something happen

It's not enough to have an idea or a solution to a problem. In isolation, an idea is worth nothing. It is only when it is put into practice that it takes on form. Something has to happen – the fourth and final stage – as a result of your creative efforts. This will require the usual planning, setting of milestones and monitoring that any implementation requires. Just because you are being creative doesn't mean that you can forget the sensible requirements of implementation. However, taking a creative approach will often mean moving further into unknown territory than usual. This calls for more of a prototyping, try something quick and fine-tune it approach, rather than planning and measuring everything to the last detail.

NOTE . . .

Prototyping is a common approach in product development and software development, but may be less familiar in other management spheres. The concept is simple. Instead of designing the finished item in its entirety, put together a mock-up, which has some of the capabilities of the final concept, but is not in any sense finished, and can be put together in a fraction of the time.

Prototypes broadly fall into three categories. Concept clarifiers are prototypes where you don't really know what you want to do. You are trying different directions with very broad-brush approximations to the real thing. Next are demonstrators, which simulate the real thing but usually aren't put together the same way. A demonstrator will give someone an idea of the look and feel of the final result, but is not in any way usable. The final type is a working subset. This is a usable product, but has only part of the functionality of the final result. It may be developed into the final result or discarded and the final result built a different way.

The point of prototyping is that it is rarely possible to specify in full detail what is required before the customer has a chance to see the finished product. By quickly achieving something like the finished product, feedback can be used to make a much closer match to the requirement. At one point most prototypes were physical, but now many (at least in the concept clarifier and demonstrator stages) are computer simulations.

I just wanted an idea

A common reaction to the Imagination Engineering framework is 'I just wanted an idea; this is overkill'. This misses the point. It is quite acceptable to use a technique out of context, or to skim through all four stages in five minutes. Equally it may be appropriate to spend several days on the process where the requirement is 'meaty' enough. The Imagination Engineering framework is a guide. It's there to use if you need it; it's there as a reminder of what you aren't doing if you don't. An important requisite for creativity is not getting bogged down in the rules. Make sure you apply that approach as much to the practice of creativity itself – use whatever looks useful, wherever it came from – as to the ideas themselves.

The creative portfolio

A first, and particularly apt, target for your creativity skills can be your portfolio. As we have already established with the obstacle map in Chapter 2, there are a number of blockages which are stopping you from achieving your dream activities. Creativity techniques are ideally suited to developing solutions to those blockages. After all, to become a chameleon manager you have to move away from the traditional way of doing things. It's no good trying to wheel out the old familiar solutions. You need something new and original. Creativity techniques can help all down the line.

Innovation in the workplace

Creativity is as appropriate to your business environment as it is to your personal portfolio. You have to be careful when letting everyone else know what you are doing, because initially they may regard creativity as odd or something outside their scope. Don't let that put you off; creativity is a powerful tool to help with big business problems. More than that – significant observers like Tom Peters have gone as far as to say that innovation is going to be the make or break factor for companies in the future. If you are going to make a success of chameleon management, you will need to be able to apply creativity in the workplace. Luckily, pretty well all the techniques are as effective being used by groups as they are by an individual.

If you are in a senior position you might like to consider how innovation can be institutionalized in your firm. Traditionally this has meant suggestion schemes and quality circles. Unfortunately, most suggestion schemes generate more bad feeling than good ideas, and quality circles are fine as far as they go, but they generally rely on experience-based inspiration without any techniques to help. Instead there are three essentials to creating a climate where creativity can flourish.

The climate for creativity

The first requirement is training. While you will have more or fewer creative staff, everyone operates well below their creative ability. Training in creativity techniques will make a huge difference.

The second requirement is a mechanism for creativity to be applied to the problems and idea generation requirements of the company. We will look at this in more detail shortly.

The third requirement is a reward system that recognizes creativity. This is not about suggestion schemes – they are creativity killers. Suggestion schemes imply that having ideas is not what your job is about. Any really creative ideas submitted are generally either ignored or implemented under the label 'part of your job, so not eligible for the scheme'. It is the small, useful but hardly creative ideas that a suggestion scheme picks up. Instead, the company's reward system must recognize the individual's creative input. This can't be done by a mechanical system. The implication is significant. A company that really fosters creativity must move away from a mechanical incentive scheme to a much more personal one. It is only where a manager is allowed to spot creativity in his or her staff and directly reward it that creativity can flourish.

This is an insidious progression. If managers are truly to have control over the rewards their staff get, they will need better training themselves to handle this process. Supporters of mechanical performance pay schemes will be up in arms by now. Surely such an approach will result in some errors? Because of malice or ignorance, some managers will pay their staff inappropriately. Absolutely. But the alternative, using the mechanical system, is that everyone is paid inappropriately, because the system doesn't and never can truly reflect the individual's contribution. It's a painful decision, and one that can only come from the top.

Creativity in groups

Creativity groups, perhaps working in fun, lunchtime sessions, are an easy way to bring people who are enthusiastic about creativity together to solve real business problems. After all, there's a huge resource in any company that is generally untapped. If you aren't senior enough to instigate this approach you could set up an informal group. It would only take one or two real hits to make the power of such groups appreciated. What's more you would also have expanded your personal portfolio.

THE CREATIVE URGE

If you are responsible for a team, you need to get the best out of them. Next time you have a team session, introduce a creativity technique, give a brief explanation of what the technique is about and try out an exercise with the team. Creativity is very different from many of the new management skills that you will be taking on. Creativity has a personal element, but the creative manager will also be a teacher, putting across creativity techniques to his or her team, encouraging the use of techniques and rewarding the results of using them.

Time bombs

The two biggest barriers to effective innovation are time and time. First, time for practice. Very few of us are taught how to be creative in school - in fact much of the education process is designed to make us less creative, encouraging pupils to come up with *the* right answer, rather than a creative answer which isn't the one the teacher thought of. As a result of this, creativity doesn't feel natural. It has been referred to as uncommon sense. For that reason, it is essential to get regular practice at using creativity techniques, both as an individual and with your team (if appropriate). This doesn't have to take up huge tranches of time, but a regular creativity slot - perhaps fifteen minutes a week to try out a technique - is necessary for success.

case study

The right answer

Stephen was enjoying his music class at junior school. The teacher played a piece of music – the '1812 Overture'. He then asked the class what it made them think of. Stephen put up his hand. 'A fox hunt, sir.' He could hear it all: the galloping horses, the horns, the animals' cries, shooting (his ideas of a fox hunt might not have been accurate, but he could hear it quite plainly). 'No, Stephen,' said the teacher. 'That's not it. What does anyone else think?' A perfectly correct answer was dismissed because it wasn't the one the teacher wanted. Stephen learned a lesson in how not to be creative – and still remembers the incident thirty years later.

The second way that time blocks creativity is the old business of 'being up to your neck in alligators'. The projects and problems where creativity is of most use are often those where time pressure is intense. No one wants to spend extra time on something secondary to the issue of solving the business problem, achieving the business goal. Yet that is how using a creativity technique will be seen – by you, by your team, by your bosses. The imperative here is to give time for creative thought the same priority as risk analysis or project planning. In fact it deserves a higher priority, but let's be realistic. Time for creative thought has to be scheduled into the process at the beginning or the outcome will be a lemming-like rush without any consideration of the alternatives.

Encouraging creativity

As the births of living creatures at first are ill-shapen, so are all innovations, which are the births of time. (Francis Bacon, sixteenth-century philosopher)

New ideas are like small green shoots. They are very easy to trample on and destroy. (A colleague of mine uses the analogy of new ideas being like new-born babies, but the picture is too grisly for me.) If you are to encourage creativity in others, you have to be aware of this. Individuals will have good ideas which they are afraid to voice because they are worried about being laughed at. To make best use of the resource that a team of people provides, you need to ensure that this does not happen – and that you do not lead the sniggering. A useful technique is de Bono's Six Thinking Hats, described in Chapter 10. The essential, though, is to give an idea some time to grow and develop before it is criticized. When you are obtaining thoughts from a team, have a moratorium on criticism and enforce it ruthlessly. Only allow comments that build on the ideas being presented.

Creativity is also something which is very dependent on mood and atmosphere. Don't expect a group of people who have just worked a gruelling ten-hour day to be full of fresh new ideas. If you really want to encourage creativity, give it a chance. Try to have ideas sessions in the morning. Be aware of the state of your group. If it is at a low-energy level, inject some energy. This can be done by using a five-minute warm-up activity, which could be as simple as getting everyone to move out of their seats. If you are working in an air-conditioned building, take everyone outside in their shirt sleeves for a couple of minutes. The fresh air will help. Throw in an energy booster like sweets or biscuits to have a quick hit on the blood sugar level and the creativity will flow.

If you have been working on a problem for some time, use a timeout to break the flow. Creativity is all about disrupting our habitual chains of thought. As well as getting everyone moving, engage in a totally different activity. Have five minutes talking about last night's television programmes, surf the Internet, read a short story – do anything that will break the pattern of thought. When you return to the problem you are much more likely to get somewhere. Just as with the time bombs section, this is a hard thing to do. When you are immersed in the thinking process, you don't want to break off, you want to continue pushing down the same line. But the break will more than repay the time spent away from the problem.

MORE INFO . . .

Managing Live Innovation by Michel Syrett and Jean Lammiman (Butterworth-Heinemann, 1998) looks in more detail at the management of business creativity.

Warming up

Warm-ups and timeouts are very helpful in creativity sessions. To be effective, they should involve physical activity and a degree of mental challenge, and should get people working together. You may have come across such activities in training sessions or as party games. If you work with a team, try to build a collection of them to liven up your thinking. This is just one example.

Step 1 *Arrange people in groups of six or eight. If the numbers don't work, some will have to watch first time around then repeat the exercise to include them.*

Step 2   *Get the groups to stand in a circle. Each person joins right hands with a person opposite. They then join left hands with another person. The aim of the exercise is to untangle the knot thus formed, leaving a ring of people holding hands, without letting go at any point (you can, of course rotate a grip).*

Result   *The resultant tangle, involving physical effort, a lot of laughter and some attempt at logic is an excellent timeout or warm-up. You can try it with other larger even-numbered groups, but with ten participants it is very difficult and with twelve practically impossible.*

Innovation to knowledge

Creativity techniques work.
Creativity requires practice.
Creativity can benefit your portfolio and your clients.

We have seen how important creativity is to the chameleon manager, and how simple techniques can be used to generate creative ideas regularly and reliably. Such innovation is not necessarily based on detailed knowledge. In fact, it is often the case that too much knowledge can be a bad thing when trying to innovate, because you will already know that it is impossible to do what you are trying to achieve, and won't bother finding a totally different way of looking at it.

For many of the challenges the chameleon manager faces, however, knowledge is an essential. Much more than the conventional manager, the chameleon manager is selling herself or himself. Having acknowledged expertise is an excellent selling point and a powerful resource when it comes to putting your talents into action. What's more in an immensely fast-changing world, keeping your knowledge up to date is an essential. Knowledge has an increasingly short shelf-life, so you had better have an excellent supplier.

THE CREATIVE URGE

6 Knowledge rules

key concept	Honing your knowledge skills.

Preview

- The three levels of data, information, knowledge.
- The conventional worker requires limited knowledge; the chameleon manager has a much broader knowledge requirement.
- Becoming an expert.
- Managing knowledge and information.
- Learning lessons from failure and building on them is part of the knowledge acquisition process.
- Taming information technology is an inescapable requirement.

Knowing it all

It is such a truism that we live in an information age that is easy to overlook the fact that most of us aren't very good at handling it. Many who were adults by the 1980s, when the personal computer came to the fore, find information technology more of a hindrance than a help. For younger managers, the technology itself is less of a problem, but information is still an uncontrollable flood. It's not just that we continue to expand the quantity of information in the world, but that we are making it easier to pour it into our lives. When I was a child, my parents were proud of the fact that we had a twenty-volume encyclopaedia to help with my education. Now I have dozens of CD-ROMs on the shelf, each of which could hold as much, plus access to the almost limitless morass of information that is the World Wide Web.

Even if you limit yourself to the old-fashioned, but still irreplaceably valuable world of books (as a writer I would say that, wouldn't I), the scope is enormous. There are around a million English language books in print in the UK and as many as twice that in the US, and of course a huge range of now unavailable works.

It wouldn't be humanly possible to know and understand even a fraction of this information. Yet whether researching a new task to expand your portfolio or finding out something for your current job, there has never been a greater need to build on your personal knowledge and be able to find an appropriate piece of information when you need it. After all, the traditional workers sold their skills up front and then largely relied on inertia and exposure to keep them in work. As a chameleon worker you will have to be constantly honing and selling your skills. Your knowledge, whatever your field, is your key asset.

Information map

Take a few minutes to draw up a mind map of your personal sources of information. Include any reference books you have around the house and at work, any media and information technology you regularly use (remember Teletext) and any sources such as libraries you make use of.

In Chapter 7 we will be expanding your information sources, for the moment it is enough to reflect on what is immediately available to you.

Data, information, knowledge

For all knowledge and wonder (which is the seed of knowledge) is an impression of pleasure in itself. (Francis Bacon, sixteenth-century philosopher)

There is a subtle gradation between data, information and knowledge, which is important to understand when considering your needs. Data is the mass of facts that you will often find in a financial report. The huge table of share prices in the daily papers is data. The numbers are immensely useful, but of themselves do nothing. It has always been easy to drown in data. In a court case a few years ago, the plaintiff produced so much data that it was estimated that it would take at least one hundred workyears to collate it to be able to do anything with it. The intention was obvious – and it wasn't to be helpful to anyone. Data is essential but risky stuff.

To be of value, data has to be analysed. The outcome of that analysis is information. In this sense, information technology is rather a pretentious term, and the old label 'data processing' is probably more accurate. Most computing is still about handling data rather than producing information. It is usually a human that will convert the data into information, and all the technology does is to distribute it. Increasingly computers can provide effective analysis, but this is still a minor role. Information is where value starts to come into the equation.

If the share prices in a newspaper are data, the commentary in the financial pages is information. Here we see why shares might be changing hands, what is happening in the business world to make the change happen. You could say that data was like words, while information was more like a story built from those words. Information is the lifeblood of the chameleon manager, and we will be looking at ways of acquiring it in the next chapter.

The final part of the progression is knowledge. This is the hardest of the three to define, except by example. In the newspaper example, knowledge is what enabled the journalist writing the article to produce the information. It combines an accumulation of information, both directly relevant and general background, and the intuition to do something with that information. Knowledge generally leaves computers standing. Although there is a branch of computer science called artificial intelligence that includes an area described as knowledge-based systems, it is not a particularly well-developed science. Knowledge-based systems try to combine information and rules to duplicate the response of a human expert, but the trouble is that all the most valuable knowledge is not really rule driven.

Rules are fine for mechanistic processes, but in business, rules have been left behind by the chaotic, frantically changing world we inhabit. Unless a business, and the people in that business, can operate freely based on a set of principles rather than being restricted to specific rules, they are unlikely to succeed any more. Knowledge is intensely valuable in this uncertain world, but rules and rules-based systems are limited to echoing the past.

A limited scope

The traditional worker had limited need for knowledge. To be fair, that's an oversimplification. Knowledge has always been the key to success, but for most people it has been of very narrow focus. If you were a good blacksmith, then you knew an awful lot about horses and their hooves, and metal-working, and fire, but very little about marketing or house-building.

With trades and professions it is quite easy to identify the scope of knowledge that is necessary. With the old picture of a manager, it's a little harder to do because, frankly, the old style of management seemed a less knowledge-based role than that of the employees. It wouldn't be stretching the point to say that most people saw their manager's role as getting in the way of getting the job done, and that the best knowledge state for this was to have practically none.

Even if you don't accept this cynical view, the traditional manager was probably not expected to have much knowledge beyond understanding people and what motivates them, and knowing how to make things happen on time. It has been trendy to consider all managers interchangeable. It doesn't matter what your firm does, you should be able to take someone with an MBA or someone with management experience elsewhere and slot them into the job.

There is a real flaw here. Even the traditional manager would benefit hugely from a good knowledge of the product base and the operation. Unless you are actually interested in what your business does, whether it's producing carpets or advertising supermarkets, you are unlikely to manage well. For the chameleon manager, though, there's even more of a knowledge challenge.

It's not British

There's a worrying aspect of the British character that says it's not good to show enthusiasm. Stiff upper lip, and all that. This suppression of enthusiasm is rife in business. Where an American businessperson wouldn't think twice about enthusing about their work, it is almost frowned on in Britain. That's a problem, because without enthusiasm, it is much harder to build knowledge.

An open world

When you begin to take charge of your own portfolio there are two big changes to your attitude to knowledge. First, it becomes a much bigger part of what you are judged on. Whether working inside a single firm or consulting for many firms, it is your expertise that will make you an attractive option for those who hold the purse strings. Secondly, your knowledge requirements will be broader. It is very rare that your dream portfolio covers only a single, well-defined area. The chameleon manager is more like the so-called 'Renaissance man' – someone who is both interested in and capable in more than one field. This is an approach that may come easier to those with a scientific background than one in the arts. If that seems a slur on arts graduates and practitioners, bear in mind that many scientists have a wide interest in the arts; few artists have a reciprocal interest.

As has already been intimated, this need to expand your knowledge base is a frightening challenge. There is so much information out there to deal with. However, given the right mechanisms for obtaining information (see Chapter 7), it is quite feasible to expand your knowledge areas without becoming overloaded. We only use a small fraction of our brains in our normal activities. Sufficient capacity is available, it is only access and time that becomes a problem. What's more, as information technology becomes more pervasive and accepted, it is less necessary that knowledge implies keeping all the appropriate information in your head. Instead, it tends more to be a matter of knowing what is available and how to access it, rather than keeping everything stored away.

It's worth noting that there is an acceptance lag here. For example, certification in the use of programming languages is often a matter of memorizing the components of the language and how they are used. This is a startling anachronism, given that these languages provide a huge amount of on-line support to the developer. There is absolutely no need to remember that in the InStr function in Visual Basic there are three parameters, the first of which is the (optional) starting position, the second the string being searched in and the third the string being searched for. Such information is presented automatically to the programmer in the development environment. It is entirely possible to be a brilliant Visual Basic programmer without ever internalizing this information. Yet the measure of 'knowledge' is still memorizing such items. The world will catch up, but inertia is strong.

Feynman's cat

Nobel Prize winning physicist Richard Feynman decided while at graduate school to attend some biology lectures for fun. Part of the course involved explaining scientific papers to classmates. Feynman was given a paper involving the muscles of a cat. As the names of the muscles meant nothing to him, he got hold of a chart to note them down. When it came to his talk he started by drawing an outline of a cat and began naming the various muscles. The other students interrupted him, telling him they knew that already.

'Oh,' said Feynman, 'you do? Then no wonder I can catch up with you so fast after you've had four years of biology.' Feynman's view: 'They had wasted all their time memorizing stuff like that, when it could be looked up in fifteen minutes.'

MORE INFO . . .

For more on Richard Feynman, see *Surely You're Joking, Mr Feynman* by Richard P. Feynman and Ralph Leighton (Vintage, 1992).

Knowledge by osmosis

If you accept that you have a wider knowledge requirement as a chameleon manager, it is necessary to do something about it. The traditional approach to knowledge acquisition was osmosis. You obtained knowledge through experience. Years of doing the job gave you lots of information about the different circumstances that could arise, allowing you to reform the information into new combinations to deal with the present day. In itself, there is nothing wrong with osmosis. However, as a chameleon manager you will need to absorb information from a wider range of sources, and to do it without the lengthy apprenticeship that used to be the norm.

One requisite is to force yourself to talk to people. This can be difficult if you are shy. It can also seem a waste of time if you are under pressure. Yet by acting as a knowledge sponge, and absorbing as much as you can from those around you, it is possible to gain a lot of essential knowledge quickly. If you look at business sectors undergoing considerable change, there is often an undercurrent of dissatisfaction among the staff. In banking, for example, where the whole business model altered in the 1990s, staff suffered considerably from enforced change. At the same time, new, younger managers were moving into bank branches. Usually they had much less experience than the staff in the bank, yet they often portrayed a stunning lack of sensitivity to the knowledge around them. They knew how to run a bank, they'd been on a training course. If they had spent more time talking to the staff – and learning from them – they would have gained both respect and valuable knowledge.

Another important requirement is taking an interest in almost anything. You never know where your next useful snippet is going to come from. Anyone who is serious about gaining knowledge but avoids appropriate sources is doing themselves no favours. 'I just don't have time to read', or 'I don't really watch television, except those wonderful animal programmes' is a recipe for limited scope.

Managed knowledge acquisition

It is certainly not necessary, and probably is risky to rely on osmosis to develop knowledge. In your specific areas of interest – and this should include all the areas in your dream portfolio, not just your current occupation – you need a managed approach to knowledge acquisition. To begin with, this is an information-collecting exercise; the information is translated into knowledge when you begin to make use of it and succeed or fail as a result, or observe others taking the same steps and what the outcomes are.

A starting point should be reading. Look at your bookshelves. How sparse are they? How many books do you have on your personal topics, and on business generally? How many of the books have been on the shelf for years? How many have you reread? To start your knowledge explosion, and you should be looking for nothing less than an explosion, set yourself a reading target. Perhaps one general business book every month and one book on a specific topic a month. Not a huge challenge, but a start. Look, too, beyond conventional textbooks. Some of the most valuable insights into business come from the crossover business and biography books which popularize, for example, how a Bill Gates has risen to fame or how an organization like the BBC has suffered disaster.

MORE INFO . . .

For some recommendations of these crossover books and a wide reading list on business and business creativity, see the on-line Creativity Unleashed bookshop at http://www.cul.co.uk/books, also accessible through the Chameleon Manager Web site http://www.cul.co.uk/chameleon.

A second source should be other people who are already involved in the particular area. Study them. How do they work? What do they do in a particular circumstance? What would you need to make yourself as attractive to would-be customers (using the term loosely to mean anyone who could provide you with work) as they are? If they are good, what makes them good? If they are bad, what should you avoid?

Finally, managed knowledge acquisition has to involve practice. Knowledge is established and reinforced by doing.

The book splurge

Step 1   *Find a bookshop with a good business section. You will probably need a real bookshop rather than a newsagent that sells books. To be a reasonable size, the business section should have at least four bookcases. With at least an hour to spare, go into the bookshop with a notebook.*

Step 2   *Go through the entire business section, looking for books that might be of interest or might develop your portfolio in a way you are interested in. Don't be put off by section titles that might not seem appropriate (for example marketing or human resource development) – categorization of books is loose at best, and you will find books that interest you in sections that aren't relevant. Don't be frightened to take books off the shelf and look at them. Be sure to include the crossover books referred to above.*

Step 3   *Each time you find a book that looks promising, note it down. Now use this list as a basis for building your library, augmented by recommendations from friends and colleagues. Recommendations are important (you might like to consider my recommendations on the Web site). While you are in the bookshop, don't come out with less than three books. Ignore the prices. Business books always seem too expensive. If you started worrying about prices, you'd never get anywhere.*

Result   *You should now have the basis for extending your library. It will be arbitrary and unfair. It will also need revisiting. But it's probably a lot better than your starting point.*

The knowledge expert

In *Honing your Knowledge Skills* (Butterworth-Heinemann, 1998), Mariana Funes and Nancy Johnson suggest that there are ten top tips for the expert knowledge manager. In the sections below, the comments are mine – they may not reflect Funes and Johnson's interpretation.

Pay attention to what your senses tell you

First, keep your eyes and ears open. Sources of information are all around you and are being missed all the time. But also remember that information is based on communication, which is inevitably flawed. To turn it into knowledge you have to filter it with your senses – the five physical senses and 'common sense'. It is necessary, though, to be aware of uncommon sense, the truth that is counter-intuitive. The fact is not everything 'makes sense' as we know it, or as our senses dictate. See 'Brain tangling' below.

Brain tangling

Probably the best example of counter-intuitive fact is the car and goats puzzle. Imagine you are a watching a game show. The contestant has to choose between three doors. Behind one is a Ferrari. Behind the other two are goats. The contestant simply has to pick a door at random. When she tells the quizmaster her choice, the quizmaster opens a different door and shows a goat. The puzzle is – should the contestant stick with the door she originally chose, should she swap to the other unopened door, or does it not make any difference to her chances of winning?

Common sense says that it doesn't matter. The quizmaster opened a door with a goat, so of the other two doors, one has a goat, the other has a car. There's a fifty-fifty chance that the car is behind either, so it doesn't matter what she does. In fact, however, the contestant should always change. That way she doubles her chance of winning. We'll look at why in a moment, but consider for a moment how unnatural this idea is. When this puzzle was first published in the newspapers, maths professors wrote in to complain that the answer was wrong. It was obviously a fifty-fifty chance.

The argument goes like this. When the contestant originally chose a door there was a one in three chance she had chosen the car. So there was a two in three chance that the car was behind one of the other two doors. All the quizmaster did was show her which of the other two doors the car wasn't behind, so there's still a two in three chance that it's behind the remaining door. For most people that doesn't make sense on the first reading. Go back and read it again. If you are still unhappy with it, be assured that many people have built computer simulations, or even done the experiment over and over again, and it really is true. It actually doubles your chances if you change choice.

Commit yourself to daily practice

Like creativity, expertise comes with repeated practice. You don't become an expert solely by reading – ever. Whatever the subjects you need to be expert in to build your personal portfolio, they require plenty of practice. When I was a manager at British Airways, most of the other managers were surprised at my expertise with a PC. They frequently wondered which courses I had attended. In fact, it was all down to experimentation and practice. Lots and lots of practice.

Turn your problems into knowledge acquisition projects

When solving problems there will be explicit information-gathering, building the background that is needed to attack the problem. But there is also the invaluable knowledge gathered during implementation. Remember that failure is the supreme learning tool. If you get everything right first time you haven't gained any real knowledge. But if you can fail fast and grow as a result of the experience, you have gained a lot. Corporate culture is generally very heavy on failure, which makes this a hard-to-use tool, but in no way lessens its value.

The valuable error

The history of business and science is littered with errors, failures and misunderstandings that have resulted in success. The gas balloon was invented by Frenchman Jacques Charles. On hearing of the Montgolfier brothers' success with a balloon, but not knowing how it worked, he mistakenly produced a whole new approach. Detergent originated when a chemist was washing out some waste material from a flask and found that it cleaned it very effectively.

Go beyond words

Words are important. Words are the basis of our civilization. Yet we can be overdependent on words. Words often make it difficult to see the 'big picture'. Obtaining a holistic view is equally necessary to having a detailed breakdown. Acquiring information through pictures and graphs, applying broad-brush models, going for underlying truths and feelings are equally valuable to the words.

Brush up on your metaphor-spotting

Metaphor is an important way of developing understanding and turning information into knowledge. It can be very useful when acquiring knowledge to think 'it's just like . . .'. All scientists take this approach. When the atom is described as consisting of a nucleus like the sun with electrons circling it like planets, metaphor is being used. No physicists believe this is what is *actually* happening, but the picture helps understanding. This approach is generally referred to in the scientific world as creating a model – not a physical model, but a conceptual model of what is happening. The danger with metaphors, however, is trying to extend your knowledge by following the metaphor. The sun and planets metaphor is useful to help understand the way an atom works, but we can't assume that other properties of planets (you can live on them, they have gravity, they can have atmospheres) apply to electrons.

Know that you already know how . . . in some context

A trifle disingenuous, this one. What is certainly true is that it is very easy to underestimate the amount of information that it is possible to find on literally any topic – especially using resources such as the World Wide Web. It is also true that there is much parallel knowledge that can be applied in a rough and ready manner. For instance, if you happened to be a butcher you will, in fact, know quite a lot about surgery. What makes it disingenuous is that few of us would like to go under that particular knife.

Reuse what you know

This simple statement is a rich source of expertise – an expert computer programmer can put together a program literally ten times faster than an average computer programmer. In part this is because of sheer native ability, but in part it will be down to a collection of code the programmer has already written which is cannibalized mercilessly to produce quick solutions. An implicit but not obvious extension to this is to use what other people know, building it into your reusable armoury. Receiving criticism is always difficult, but if you can accept a constructive statement from someone else about the way you do something, you can reuse that to great effect.

Of course you can do it, but do you want to?

Expertise is not just knowing what to do, but also what not to do. Simple as that (if only).

Go for simplicity: do what works!

Pragmatism is stunningly effective. Too often we are frustrated by a lack of match to our exact requirement. Taking what works and using it, rather than waiting for perfection is a classic mark of the expert. Without knowledge you can take a woodworker's workshop tools and be unable to turn out a single piece of furniture. With knowledge you can produce something wonderful given minimal tools. Simplicity itself is a mark of expertise. Good design, for example, can be quite fussy – great design is usually very simple.

Don't aspire to be a magpie

This is one of those infuriating statements that is both true and false at the same time. In collecting information, in building your knowledge, it is easy to become a magpie. The magpie collects facts and expertise in an area that looks shiny and exciting, without any idea of application. It is certainly much better to be focused in your knowledge acquisition. No one can be an expert in every field. However, it is useful to be a magpie when it comes to items such as your contact database. Magpie behaviour works when collection of information is quick, storage is in a form you can quickly retrieve, like a computer database, and the information doesn't inhibit your memory once stored.

'Great, I got it wrong!'

It's time to make use of failure in this short activity.

Step 1   *Think back to the last time you made a real mess of something, but ignore anything in the last month. Very recent events are still too fresh; you want to be able to remember the detail of what happened, but not to feel too stupid about it any more.*

Step 2   *Note down what you learned as a result of what went wrong, and whatever happened to limit the damage and/or fix the outcome.*

Result   *This was your learning from a single event. The chances are some or all of these fragments of knowledge would not be ones that you would have picked up without the failure. No one is saying that you ought to go out of your way to fail, but a fast acceptance of the lessons followed by a quick, fresh start is the only way to proceed.*

The holey pipes

A few years ago I was irritated by the creaking of a floorboard on the way into the bathroom. One day I decided to do something about it and nailed it down. The first nail didn't hold it firm enough. As I banged in a second nail, a stream of black, warm water shot out from the hole in the floorboard. I had penetrated a pipe. Hurriedly I turned off the water and levered up the board. As the first nail came out, a second stream of water shot up. Both nails had gone through a pipe. What's more, turning the water off had no immediate effect. I had nailed through a central heating pipe.

The next half hour was one of the worst I can remember, with blackened walls, ceiling cracking below and general chaos. Yet looking back, I have gained a surprising amount of knowledge. Don't do this sort of work with no one else in the house. Don't just nail through floorboards without checking what's under them. Stick the nails back in the holes if you do it (I didn't spot this until most of the system was drained). And, thanks to the plumber, stop creaking floorboards by bedding them in sealant. Not a way of learning lessons I'd like to repeat, but certainly a powerful one.

Making information technology work for you

In Chapter 7 we will look at how and where to acquire information, but to build knowledge it helps to be comfortable with the means of disseminating information. For a long time this has meant being able to read and write, but that is no longer enough. Information technology is now as much a part of business life as paper and pen. As a chameleon manager, you cannot excuse yourself from the information revolution. If you are comfortable with personal computers and software, fine – but all too many managers are either wary of these essential tools of the trade or consider them the business of the secretary. Forget that – the secretary's role is becoming extinct.

I am not suggesting that you need to be a computer expert, but there are some basic skills which would greatly repay the effort to learn them. First and most basic is typing and mouse skills. While there are now products which can accept dictation and translate it on to the computer screen, they still trip up regularly, and are of limited use for anything but pouring words in. As a chameleon manager you more than others are likely to be measured on the quality of your output. This means that material you produce should look good and be written in an approachable manner. For most of us this means a fair amount of editing, which is only practically performed with mouse and keyboard. While it might be excessive to do a full touch-typing course, using a software-based tutor until you can type without looking at the keyboard will be well worth the effort.

KNOWLEDGE RULES

Similarly you should get to know the basic software that you use. Explore your word processor, spreadsheet, Web browser . . . whatever you use as day-to-day business software. Go beyond what you've always done: you will find facilities hidden away that will make your life much easier. Try out any on-line tutorials or guides. Most of all, don't be afraid to experiment. The prime difference between the PC generation who were brought up with personal computers, and older users is that they will plunge in and try something. Fear of embarrassment (make sure you can have a go without someone looking over your shoulder) and breaking something (you won't – the worst you can do is lose some data, and that's easy enough to avoid) hold so many people back from achieving all the benefits of using a personal computer.

This book isn't about using a PC. If you'd like more help there are plenty of guides around. However, there is one more requirement that is absolutely essential for the chameleon manager that might not have seemed so important before: backing up. If you are producing anything of relevance to your portfolio on your PC, whether it's your CV, a report for a client or a novel, it wouldn't be much fun if you lost it. Use Windows-based backup software (avoid DOS Backup, in my opinion it's a nightmare) to save your information on to floppy disks if there's not much. Alternatively there are now plenty of media with greater capacity. Tape, high-volume diskettes, and rewriteable CDs are all making it easier to keep your essential data safe. You ought to back up (i.e. make a safe copy of your work) every night. It's also handy to have an occasional exchange of backups with someone at a different location. That way, in the unlikely event (as they say on aircraft) of your office burning down, you won't lose everything.

Now you know, how do you get information?

Knowledge is essential to the chameleon manager.
You will sell yourself on expertise.
Failure is an excellent tutor.
A good grasp of information technology is necessary.

We have identified knowledge as one of the key differentiators of the chameleon manager. Knowledge is more than data – a simple set of numbers or facts – and more than information – the analysis or interpretation of such data. Knowledge is the ability to generate information and make use of it. When managing your own portfolio you are more likely to be judged on your knowledge – your expertise – and you will need a broader range of knowledge to cope with your wider portfolio.

In the next chapter we will consider how to gather the information that will underlie your knowledge, using conventional sources and the newer possibilities which information technology opens up.

7 Information location

key concept | Honing your knowledge skills.

Preview

● Finding information to broaden your knowledge.
● Unearthing conventional sources of information.
● A basic reference shelf.
● Using the World Wide Web.
● Using Internet newsgroups.
● Searching the Web.

Obtaining information

You need information, to build your knowledge base and for specific projects. Because you are likely to have a wider focus and, because you may have less company resources to support you, you need to become expert at information location. Traditionally this has meant scouring the libraries, and they still have their place, but it would be foolish now to ignore the power and accessibility of the Internet.

In Chapter 6 there was an activity mapping your current reference sources. As we explore ideas in this chapter, why not add them to your map for future reference.

Libraries and reports

It is easy to underestimate libraries. A good city or university library still provides an excellent source for research, but habit has restricted many of us to using small, very local libraries to provide fiction (particularly for children) and very little else. Much of this chapter will focus on alternatives to the library, and it's probably fair to say that it has now become the fall-back rather than the prime research source, but the library should not be forgotten.

An alternative paper source is the report. There are plenty of companies where very intelligent people spend their time collating information in reports to sell on. Such research organizations cover practically every area of business and technology. In general I am a little doubtful about them as a source of speculative information, as the reports tend to be expensive, and similar but more concise opinions can be gained for little or nothing from the press. However, where a report is, for example, summarizing the current state of a particular business it can be an excellent way to get up to speed quickly.

Report in action

Roger was a consultant, helping a number of companies link their telephone exchanges to computers. He had a lot of experience on the computer side, but was relatively new to telephony. He bought a report on computer/telephony integration from an established source. A minor point which this report brought out was the risk of reliance on caller ID. This feature enables the recipient to identify the telephone number of the caller, and Roger had planned to use it to route incoming calls. However, the report identified that, at the time, many business calls did not provide caller ID information as there was poor integration between company private exchanges and the public network. They generally weren't capable of giving out a direct dial number, so gave out 'UNAVAILABLE' instead. This information enabled Roger to save three projects from very expensive problems at a later date by changing the way that callers were identified.

On the shelf

Once you would have needed access to a library to get general background information from a good encyclopaedia. Unless you were prepared to pay four-figure sums to have a full set of books, it meant a trek to the library each time. Now, however, with full-sized encyclopaedias available on CD-ROM for little more than the price of a game, it's arguable that an encyclopaedia should form part of the chameleon manager's reference shelf alongside a good dictionary.

Apart from such essentials that are liable to be of use for anyone, your reference shelf may need other works. Many businesses have yearbooks or guides that can be invaluable – for example, anyone writing for any audience should have an up-to-date copy of at least one of the writers' handbooks giving not only advice but addresses and details of publishers, magazines, broadcasters and other potential customers.

Managing the media

Depending on the nature of your portfolio, newspapers and trade journals can be an important source of information. Increasingly this information is available in electronic form. Sometimes you can access printed sources on the Internet, but often the content is restricted. A useful approach that many publishers now take is to bring out newspapers and magazines on CD-ROMs. Usually you will get one or more years' output for a surprisingly reasonable fee. The big advantage of an electronic version is that they are fully searchable. No more browsing through page after page with a microfilm reader, you can jump immediately to the relevant articles. If particular publications are of importance to you, consider investing in the CD-ROM version.

INFORMATION LOCATION

What's on CD?

Step 1   *Identify half a dozen prime sources of information that would be valuable to you. These might be yearbooks, trade press, encyclopaedias, dictionaries, national press etc. It doesn't matter whether you use them at the moment or not.*

Step 2   *Find out if these sources are available on CD-ROM. If it isn't obvious, ring them up and ask them. There are few if any sources of information who object to this sort of question. Find out what it would cost to have your core library on CD-ROM.*

Result   *Your core library may not all be available on CD-ROM, but a proportion of it will be. It is worth giving serious consideration to adopting CD-ROM where the source is one that requires more than simple searching. For instance a dictionary of quotations or a magazine or newspaper is much easier to search in its electronic form.*

Plugging into the Web

There has never before been a source of information like the World Wide Web, the friendly face of the Internet where pages of information, pictures, sound and video can be quickly explored using hypertext links. For a long time it was possible to ignore the Web and hope it would go away. If you didn't like technology it was quite legitimate to argue that it consisted of piles of obscure information that no one would ever require, interspersed with pornography and trivia. All of that is still there, but there is now a richness about the Web that has turned it into the ultimate reference source.

Part of the reason for this is that commercial companies have leaped on to the Web and are supplying large amounts of information for free. Equally powerful is the input of the small contributor. On any subject from Doctor Who to

Transylvanian Bare-necked chickens, there are liable to be experts and enthusiasts. There's a natural urge when you are an expert to share your knowledge. The Web gives you a chance to publish for free (almost) to a potential audience of millions. Okay, in practice few people will look at a site on the breeding habits of the tuna, but you have made your small contribution. This ability to tap into a planet-wide source of expertise is remarkable and unparalleled. Of course, it is necessary to exert some judgement – not all self-styled experts know what they are talking about – but this does not invalidate the Web as a source.

If you are already a World Wide Web user, both at work and at home, you can skip the rest of this section. If you only use it in one of those locations (or neither of them), stick with me. Let's deal with the home first, as it's easier. It isn't enough to have Web access in the office, partly because of timeliness, partly because you will want to use it for parts of your portfolio that aren't to do with that particular job and partly because there's something restrictive about using the Web with someone looking over your shoulder. Web access from home involves having a PC (if you don't own a PC check back with the previous chapter – you need one), a modem or faster connection method (ISDN, cable modem, lots of other fancy initials) and a service provider. The Internet, where the World Wide Web resides, is simply an unstructured collection of computers linked together. To be part of the Internet needs more resources than most of us operate from home, so instead we connect over a telephone line to a service provider, someone who does have computers which are permanently part of the Internet. The service provider forms a route into the network.

At one time getting such a connection set up was quite difficult; these days it's generally relatively easy. At the end of the process you should be able to jump anywhere on the World Wide Web (fairly slowly if you are using a modem), pursuing whatever topic you require. Of course, the Web is a vast unstructured morass of information and data – we'll be looking later in this chapter at how to navigate it. You will use the Web as a major resource for your work; as such, the connection charges are simply a working cost, and you should consider them such alongside your PC, car or whatever, not as a frightening overhead.

You may have little control over whether or not you have access to the Web at work, but ought to push for it if it isn't available. Businesses can provide constant access at high speeds, making the Internet even more useful as an immediate reference source.

Soil on the Web

To demonstrate the effectiveness of the Web, I entered 'Soil Science' into one of the search engines (UK Infoseek). Among the first ten entries were:

- the Reading Centre for Earth and Atmospheric Sciences, with details of research, courses and seminars and pointers to other soil science sites
- the Soil Micromorphology Newsletter
- the personal home page of an agronomist
- details of a computer-based course in land literacy
- desertification research

. . . and many, many more entries followed.

There's more to the Internet

If you listened to or read only the popular media, you would think that the Internet and the World Wide Web were interchangeable terms. In fact, the Web is only part of the Internet. A major part, it's true, but not the whole thing. Bearing in mind that the Internet is only a collection of interconnected computers, the Web is simply one set of information on it. The Internet also acts as the transmission medium for most of the electronic mail that flies around the world. It provides homes for less flashy information sources like Internet newsgroups, which are on-line bulletin boards discussing a particular topic (tens of thousands of them), and FTP sites, effectively libraries of computer files. Increasingly, also, the Internet plays host to live connection between individuals, either via typed-in chat sessions or through Internet phones which enable low-quality spoken voice to accompany pictures and whiteboard-like communication at local call costs anywhere in the world.

Newsgroups particularly are likely to be of use to the chameleon manager. They work rather like putting electronic mail onto a bulletin board that anyone can see. Don't be afraid to explore newsgroups. Unlike a chat session, the other users can't see you – you can have a look round without being noticed or contributing (known to newsgroup users as lurking). The real value of newsgroups is that they are a discussion medium on a closely defined topic. If you need to know more about connecting a palmtop PC to your desktop, or cooking bagels, or . . . well practically anything, you are likely to find a newsgroup discussing it. You can use it passively, simply looking out for someone with the information you need, or actively, posting an entry to the newsgroup with a request for help.

There's a lot said about Internet etiquette (netiquette), and the practice of flaming – pouring vitriolic replies on someone who says the wrong thing. Mostly, netiquette is common sense. Newsgroups have regular contributors who can form a clique, but they are usually eager to help as long as your question isn't aggressive. Tell them their pet subject is rubbish, and don't be surprised if you get an unpleasant reply, but ask for help politely and you can get excellent results.

NOTE . . .

Although use seems to be decreasing as the Internet opens up, it is not uncommon, particularly in on-line chat services and newsgroups, to see contractions used. This practice dates back to Morse code, where the need to spell everything out in dots and dashes led to various code phrases, for example QRM and QRN as man-made and natural interference respectively. Internet communications involve both contractions and a means of putting a tone or emotional weighting on a piece of text. Best known are the rather twee emoticons, e.g. :) to indicate a smile accompanying the text. Others are contractions like BG for big grin, or ROFL for roll on the floor laughing. Use them sparingly, but be aware that others might use them. Full lists are generally available on Internet service providers' sites.

One thing that isn't obvious when you first encounter newsgroups is that the content is transient. Where a Web page will stay in place as long as the owner wants it to and continues to pay for the site (bizarrely, there are now services which look after a Web site after the owner's death), newsgroup entries (referred to as postings) only remain for a

INFORMATION LOCATION

short period of time. The duration depends on the popularity of the newsgroup, but a typical lifetime would be between two weeks and two days. This is necessary to avoid newsgroups eating up disk space, but means that you will often find that discussions seem disjointed, as you will see answers without the original questions, and there is a danger of asking a question that has been asked a hundred times before, which may irritate regular users of the newsgroup. If you feel that a newsgroup is going to be of long-term use, the software used to read the groups can usually save content off-line (i.e. while not connected to the Internet), helping you maintain the whole discussion. Frequently asked questions (shortened to FAQs) are often kept available to avoid the embarrassment of re-asking. Check these before posting a query.

A final source that is increasingly popular is 'push' information. This is information which is actively sent to you, rather than information you have to go and look for. The simplest form is the e-mail news service. The idea here is that you subscribe to a service (often free unlike a magazine subscription), which then sends regular e-mails to you on the subject of your choice. Such services are usually joined from Web sites. If there is a service around your topic of interest (or general news), you may find this a very convenient way to keep up to date. Such services often have links to Web sites to expand on subjects which are useful to you.

A more sophisticated form of push is the Web channel. Here your PC maintains a special version of a Web site locally. On a regular basis – once an hour, once a day, once a week, depending on your inclination – the PC connects to the Internet and is sent any new information that is relevant to this Web site. This approach is referred to as a channel, like a TV channel, and is presented with a lot of gloss, but in principle it is a simple technique and one that again can ensure that you always have the latest information to hand.

There is a problem to all this. The Internet wasn't designed to take the traffic it does. Nothing could have been – the growth has simply been beyond anyone's imagination. In its original beginnings as ARPANET, the Internet was a means of linking research establishments, mostly US universities, involved in defence research. Later, with the invention of the Web at the European CERN research centre, and with the explosive growth of e-mail, it became a much more consumer-oriented facility. The Internet is permanently under threat of collapse as more and more is loaded on it. In practice, although it can sometimes be painfully slow, the frantic work to shore up and expand the capacity of the Internet always seems to keep up somehow. There is a nominal risk that the whole thing will collapse, but the pragmatic evidence is that it won't.

MORE INFO . . .

The way the commercial growth of the Internet affected the main software companies, and particularly Microsoft, is covered very enjoyably in *OverDrive* by James Wallace (John Wiley, 1997).

Needles in haystacks

Having decided you want to use the World Wide Web as an information resource, you have the problem of finding what you want. Although it is eminently resolvable, the depth of this problem shouldn't be underestimated. Remember the picture of a Web site as a noticeboard in a huge field. Somewhere in the field there will almost certainly be a board with the information you want, but where? There are literally millions of boards. There is no real structure. Anyone can add a board anywhere in the field whenever they like, or take one down. A board can be so big that you need binoculars just to see the edges of it. It makes the traditional problem of finding a needle in a haystack seem an exercise for beginners.

Before you give up in distress, though, the Web has mechanisms to help. The underlying structure of the Web indicates this. In fact, the very picture of a Web is telling. There are strands that link different pages, different sites together. Once you find something about your subject of interest, you may well find links to other useful sites. The Chameleon Manager site (http://www.cul.co.uk/chameleon) is a good example. You will find many links to other, helpful sites. So at least, with our noticeboards in a field model, you can follow a piece of string that will lead you to another relevant noticeboard, if you can find a useful noticeboard in the first place.

INFORMATION LOCATION

Equally valuable are search engines. The Web has no structure. It can't have a formal contents page or index like a traditional reference work. But it is possible, with a lot of effort, to keep looking around the Web and noting new things. Search engines generally have computers dedicated to gliding around the Web, looking for sites to add to their listings. They come in two forms, the straightforward index and the structured list by type of site. In either case, however, you will be able to type in something that you are interested in searching for and get a response.

Problem solved? Not entirely. Any particular search engine (there are plenty of them – check the Chameleon Manager site for recommendations) will miss huge chunks of the Web at any one time. Often, you will find a popular topic has so many possible responses that what comes back from the search engine is almost as overwhelming as the Web itself. You can refine your search by adding more details or using the advanced features of the search engine. Don't be put off by the word 'advanced' – often this just means that you can more easily specify that the entry should contain a particular phrase but not something else, or similar mechanisms to make your search results more relevant.

Bear in mind, when using a search engine that you are communicating with a computer, which will interpret what you type absolutely literally. If your search fails, check for spelling mistakes. Consider different ways the subject you are searching for may be referred to. Let's say you were researching vets in Ireland. You might get quite different results looking for 'vet', 'veterinary', 'veterinary surgeon', 'veterinary hospital', 'animal doctor', 'pet doctor' and so forth. Using a search engine takes a little patience, but is well worth the effort.

Engines in action

Step 1

Take a subject you need information on, for work, for a hobby or for your social life. Find four or five different search engines (you can find them on the Chameleon Manager site) and try your topic in each. Make sure at least one of the engines is specific to your country.

Step 2   *Compare the first couple of pages of response. See how the results vary. If you are searching for a phrase rather than a single word try entering it in different ways. For example, if you were looking for rubber gloves, you might try:*

○   *rubber gloves*
○   *"rubber gloves"*
○   *+rubber +gloves.*

In some (but not all) search engines, putting the search term in double inverted commas will find only that phrase, while starting each word with + will find entries which have all the words in (but not necessarily together). If the subject you are covering is sometimes shortened, try both the initials and the full term.

Result   *This is a knowledge-gaining activity, rather than one to generate specific information. It's not so much to tell you which engines to use, as each will be better at different topics. Nor is it to research rubber gloves (or whatever you chose). It is the first stage in getting a feel for how different ways of using different search engines result in different outcomes.*

Your personal information magnet

If search engines aren't delivering for you, there's a further step you can take. For a small cost you can get search manager software for your PC. This software will go out to various search engines, look for your information, then check the links, summarizing the pages so that you can quickly sort the useful pages from the irrelevant. Software comes and goes with worrying rapidity – see the Chameleon Manager Web site (http://www.cul.co.uk/chameleon) for specific details.

The big advantage of using a search manager is that it overrides many of the traditional problems with search engines. It will use several different engines, to overcome the fact that each engine has blind spots, areas of the Web it doesn't handle well. It enables you to search on more than

INFORMATION LOCATION

one term at once, so you can cover the different ways your item might have been referred to. And it summarizes what is actually on the pages, eliminating the frustrating trawl through pages that have either disappeared entirely or have nothing to do with your topic.

A search manager will take much longer to perform a search than a single engine as it is visiting the sites as well as the search engines, but in terms of quality and lack of time wasted sifting through the outcome, the results are well worth the extra connection time.

Information and communication

key concept

Information is an essential.
Build a reference shelf.
The World Wide Web should be one of your tools.
There's more to the Internet than the Web.

Information is not nice to have, it's essential. The more you take charge of your own portfolio, the more you will have to take charge of your own information sourcing. Conventional means like libraries will give some benefits, but this is an area where you cannot afford to be a Luddite and stay away from information technology. The Internet, particularly in the form of the World Wide Web, provides an unparalleled source of information accessible twenty-four hours per day (systems permitting) from the comfort of your home or office.

In this chapter we looked at the search engines and managers that can help find the appropriate information, but such low-level, one-way communication is only part of your need to bridge the gap. Communications are the lifeline of the chameleon manager – making sure that they work well is a make or break issue, as we will examine in the next chapter.

8 It's good to talk

key concept | Managing network relationships.

Preview

- You can't work in isolation.
- Growing your network and keeping it healthy is essential for the chameleon manager.
- Using conventional communication tools.
- Getting leverage from electronic mail.
- The many barriers to communication.
- Developing quality communication.

Working from a garret

We are entering a new age of the independent worker. It is quite possible to consider the twentieth century, with its focus on large company employment, as a historical oddity. Most civilized human experience has been of individuals or small groups of people working together. However, just because we are moving back to a more independent picture does not mean that we are taking on all the disadvantages that the old independents had. As a chameleon manager, even if you move to a full, self-managed portfolio, you are not going to be working in isolation in a garret. It doesn't make sense commercially or socially.

Instead you will need to make use of others to provide contacts, information and the various elements which will comprise your new working environment. We have already considered the importance of your network to finding work, but this chain continues right through delivering the work to closing off and getting paid.

DisOrganized working

The interdependence you will rely on as a chameleon manager is reflected in the changing way that companies are organizing. In a book entitled *DisOrganization*, I argue together with co-author Paul Birch that successful companies will need to become more like a network of small companies, each sized no larger than fifty to a hundred entities. These minicompanies will operate independently, but be contracted to fulfil the goals of a linking company, called a netcompany. The netcompany's role will be to set the direction and provide excellent communications between the minicompanies.

The overall entity which is working together, we call a hypercompany. This consists of the netcompany, a number of minicompanies which are within the same ownership, but also a number of minicompanies which have either been spun off, or never were part of the same organization. These traditionally would be partners or suppliers. This gives a picture of the new type of company that's something like the illustration provided on p. 119.

MORE INFO...

See *DisOrganization* by Brian Clegg and Paul Birch (Pitman, 1998) for a full description of the new style of company.

It is absolutely essential to grasp this business model, because it shows exactly how a chameleon manager functions. When you have established your own portfolio, you become a one-person minicompany, whether or not you actually establish yourself as a limited company. If you choose to remain a dedicated employee with a wider portfolio outside work, you are one of the minicompanies that are solely within the hypercompany that is your employer. If you begin to perform other tasks while still with the employer, you become one of the minicompanies within the large hypercompany which also have links out to another netcompany. If you set up on your own, supplying services to one or more other companies, you become an external minicompany, linking into other hypercompanies.

The problem you will have with this approach is that many companies will not have adopted the hypercompany/minicompany/netcompany structure. They will still be a monolithic lump with a 'them and us' mentality. This doesn't mean that you will stop employing a minicompany approach, but that you need to do it less explicitly and more cautiously.

ABB

DisOrganization is a relatively new concept, so there are relatively few real-life cases yet. Probably the best example is the Scandinavian engineering giant, ABB, a favourite of business guru Tom Peters. The remarkable ABB chief Percy Barnevik runs his 200,000 or more people operation with only 150 central staff. The rest of the organization is split into 5,000 units, averaging forty people each. Each unit operates as if it was its own business, with all the benefits of a small business's focus and energy.

Growing your network

In an activity in Chapter 3 you examined your current network, but a network is an organic thing, constantly changing to meet your new needs. Growing your network should be a constant background activity. If you receive a letter or see something interesting in a magazine, take five minutes to bring the person involved into your network. Add them to your network database and get in touch. If a useful contact is mentioned when doing a job, take a note of it and look at how you can follow it up. Always be prepared to add to your network, even people who perhaps seem quite peripheral to your needs at the moment: you don't know when and how they can be of use in the future.

Nurturing your network

If a network is organic, it will need nurturing. This takes two forms, pruning and fertilizing. Every now and then you need to prune your network. Although I strongly recommend the magpie approach of adding everyone who may possibly be of use in the future, information does become out of date and irrelevant. On an infrequent but regular basis – perhaps twice a year – it pays to search through your network database and throw out the obvious 'dead wood'. One good time of year to do this is over the Christmas/New Year period, when (work) demands on your time are often light.

More significant is fertilizing. Simply adding names to your database only establishes a very limited link into your network. Yes, you have a name, which will minimize effort if you do need to get in touch, but there is only so much that you can do with a name alone. Another regular activity, perhaps twenty minutes a week, should be nurturing your network by making contact. If you have someone you haven't dealt with before, see if there is some way you can get in touch that will be to their advantage. Just a phone call, or a letter or e-mail that will register in their mind that you are a potentially useful contact (remember that networks work both ways).

For existing contacts who know you, try to keep track of when you last spoke or e-mailed. If you aren't in contact a couple of times in a year, they have dropped back to the level of handy names – consider whether some new dialogue would be valuable. Finally, your active contacts, the ones that are actually providing you with work, need the strongest fertilizing (make sure, though, that you don't use bullshit: this simply doesn't work as a fertilizer). Is there some opportunity for a face-to-face contact? Look beyond the traditional. There's nothing wrong with a Christmas card, but business Christmas cards have become so much of a ritual that they have no real value. Try instead to take them for a drink, or send them something you have spotted that might be of interest to them.

The electronic little black book

I have already mentioned the need for a network database to keep track of your network. Now I'd like to specifically recommend that you keep this in an electronic form. What's wrong with a Rolodex or address book? Quite a lot. In an old-fashioned job, your network was less important and changed much more slowly. For a chameleon manager it would not be surprising if 50 per cent of your network changed every year or so. New people are always being added; existing people's details change constantly. What's more, the size of your network database is liable to be larger than a typical address book. I currently have over 500 entries in my contacts file, and my range of contacts is quite limited.

The sheer flexibility of an electronic address book is the first advantage. To keep it up to date, I would also give serious consideration to having an electronic organizer or palmtop PC. These tiny computers have limited functionality, but are eminently portable. An electronic address book is useless if it is sitting in the PC on your desk and you are in a different town or country. However, before buying a handheld device, make sure that there is easy interchange of information with your chosen means of storing contact details. Don't rely on the advertisement; it is often misleading, talking about what is theoretically possible, without mentioning that you need to buy someone else's product, or to wait until next year when the new version of the software is available. Make sure you actually see it working before you buy. If the store can't demonstrate it, you've a good argument for buying somewhere else.

With your network details on both PC and palmtop you are equipped to act wherever you are, whenever you need a contact. Other reasons for going electronic? It's easy to tie in not just telephone numbers and addresses but all the burgeoning means of communication. You should be able to store fax numbers, e-mail addresses and more in your electronic little black book and use them directly without retyping (something else you should check out before settling on a product). Electronic contact databases will also allow you to make cross-references to documents and notes, or to link contacts to your diary and task list. Electronic support makes good sense for the sort of network you are likely to need.

Your black book

If you don't have an electronic little black book, set one up before undertaking this activity. If you have one and it is already perfectly structured you won't have much to do.

Step 1   *Try to do the following. Extract a list of names to do with one of your personal portfolio topics. Get a second list of people you have not seen for over a year. Extract a final list of people who might be relevant to the first item on your top ten concerns this week.*

Step 2   *Imagine you had to write a letter to everyone on the first list of names, make telephone calls to all on the second and send an e-mail to everyone the third. What would you do?*

Result   *The second step should give you an impression of how effective your little black book technology is. Good organizer software should allow you to mail merge into your word processor, set up a list of calls or send e-mails. If you don't know how to do any of these, spend a little time finding out if and how it is possible. Mail merge, for example, still has a nasty reputation from the days when it was a baffling, unsupported process. Now it is practically as easy to address a letter to twenty people as it is to one.*

The first step should clarify the quality of your data. If your organizer software doesn't note your last contact, you can make a note of it in the free notes section. Linking individuals to topics can be achieved in a number of ways. If you regularly contact a set of individuals on a subject you can set up a mailing list of people from your little black book. Searches can check for text in the notes field, or you can set up topics as categories or keywords which you add to each entry in the book.

Managing phone and fax

Just because there is a lot of focus in this book on the newer means of communication, it does not mean that old favourites like the phone and fax have lost their value. The phone, particularly, remains an essential tool. If your style of chameleon management is as an independent, you will need a separate business phone, and probably a mobile phone too. Although the mobile phone became a yuppie icon in the 1980s and early 1990s, it is too valuable a resource to be ignored. Fax is still useful, but is losing its importance as e-mail becomes more prevalent. Even so, it will remain a valuable tool well into the twenty-first century. At the very least, you should ensure that the modem used to connect your computer for e-mail and Web access can also function as a fax. Although this hasn't the flexibility of a dedicated fax machine, it will be there when you need it.

The phone is now so ubiquitous that it might seem offensive to make suggestions on how to use it. After all, we all know how to work a phone. However, the technology behind the handset has moved on so quickly, and the approach to using the phone is so important that it is worth spending a moment on it. Phones can be extremely intrusive, so a first inclination might be to always have your voice mail or telephone answering machine switched on. This is a disaster. Certainly use some means of capturing a message if you aren't there, but don't hide behind it. Your callers aren't stupid. After a few failed attempts to get through they will realize what is happening, and some simply won't bother to call you any more.

It is much better to answer the phone, despite the interruption this causes, but be prepared to politely reschedule the conversation if it is liable to be long and hinder an important task. You can help other people into the same position by always asking them if they've the time for a five-minute (or whatever) chat at the start of your conversaton with them. That way, if you caught them as they were dashing out or about to start a meeting they can tell you to call another time without being embarrassed.

When it comes to making calls, you can apply much more structure. Calls spread through the day break up your work. If you think of someone you have to call, don't do it immediately, unless there's a burning reason to do so. Jot it down on your calls list and make it in a block of time you allocate for the task, perhaps twice a day.

The key technological advancements to consider lie in the electronic exchanges which most large companies and telecommunication providers use. What do you do if you ring someone and they are engaged? Either you keep trying or you try to remember to call back later, only realizing that you haven't well after office hours. BT and others now provide a service to call you back when the line is free. Although a service like this has a cost attached to it, it is far outweighed by the amount of your time that would be wasted performing the function yourself. Consider also the caller ID service, which displays the caller's number before you pick the phone up. This is particularly valuable if your phone or PC can link the number to a name, showing you who is likely to be calling. Many business exchanges unfortunately do not provide caller information to the network, so you will find a reasonable number of business calls will not be identified. The service is still worth considering, though, not so much to give the person at the other end a shock when you greet them by name, as to allow you to make some quick decisions – should I find some information, should I switch on the voice mail – before answering.

Caller ID

Caller ID only began to be supported by UK PC modems in 1997, and had a very gradual take-up. However, if you have a modem that does support it there are lots of exciting possibilities. When you get a voice mail message, it could automatically record the caller's number. When you get an incoming call it could look up the number in your little black book and flash up the entry. You could even program a voice mail system to handle calls from different numbers in a different way. Even more a shame, then, that the number is quite frequently unavailable. Note that in the UK you have to pay to have the caller ID information made available to you. Frankly, this seems criminal: it ought to be a right.

Call waiting, the service that allows you to hold a second incoming call while already on the line, has its proponents, but it is more risky than most of the options. If you decide not to pick up the new call, it is irritating for the person calling, as they will have been told that you know they are waiting and will then have ignored them. What's more, the call back when free service fails to work in this circumstance, which is doubly frustrating for the caller. Call waiting also means that your calls are likely to be disrupted. It is probably better to get a mechanism whereby calls are diverted either to a second line or to voice mail when you are busy. In fact, diversion in general is a particularly handy service. If you are expecting an urgent call and have to go out, you can divert it through to your mobile phone and the caller gets seamless access. What's more, if you have caller ID and it is available on the call, it will be diverted through to your mobile phone. If you don't have appropriate equipment, consider using the voice mail service that most telecommunication providers offer. It is often more flexible than an answering machine.

The electronic mail explosion

Just as the World Wide Web has transformed information gathering, electronic mail (e-mail) brings communication into a new dimension. E-mail is not a substitute for paper or the phone, but it expands your information capabilities in a very dramatic way. Originally mostly found locally within an organization, e-mail via the Internet has opened up as a worldwide communication medium.

The benefits of e-mail are worth exploring. The first is non-urgent immediacy. If you need to speak to someone *now*, e-mail is not the answer. But for anything else, you can put a note together in a couple of minutes and dispatch it. The job is done. There is a double benefit. Not only have you communicated, but also you have mentally ticked the task off. This is extremely important. The brain can only cope with a limited number of parallel tasks. If you are worried about having to communicate to someone, this need will effectively be blocking a channel, decreasing your efficiency. By sending off an e-mail you can consider the action to be taken, drop the need from your short-term memory and free up scarce resources.

The other big benefit of e-mail is the ability to include attachments. Not only can you send a note, you can send a computer file – a program, a document, a spreadsheet – whatever you need. This is immensely valuable if you are working remotely with a company as you can share information, develop documents, generally work together without the need for time-consuming physical transport.

E-mail in action

● I have co-written three books with another author. We live about an hour's drive apart. Not an impossible distance, but one we don't particularly want to cover unless we have to. E-mail has been absolutely central to our development of the books. Each of us writes a chapter, then exchanges it with the other to build on it. During final polishing, the whole book is flying back and forth on an almost daily basis. A book occupies a fair amount of disk space – perhaps a megabyte – which means it takes a little longer for the phone call than a normal e-mail message, but compare it with the alternative. Not only would exchanging manuscripts by post have at least a three-day turnround, the costs of printing and postage would be much greater.

● Martin develops software for a major corporate, but is based a hundred miles away. Although he travels in once a fortnight for a half-day of meetings, all other communication is managed by e-mail and phone. Specifically, any documents and changes to the program code are sent by e-mail. This way it is possible for a problem to be fixed and the customer to be working again before Martin could even have arrived if he had instead set out by car.

● Sue runs a large project, using project management software to support and monitor the process. Each week she issues update requests directly from her software. These are carried by e-mail to her staff, who update electronic forms directly on their PCs. The information then slots back automatically into her project management package. Sue also makes use of e-mail for almost all her day-to-day administration. It hasn't replaced personal contact with her team, but she can now make better use of that limited time to address issues and generate ideas, rather than waste it in administration.

There are some dangers to e-mail. If you are working remotely, using a telephone connection, it is easy to forget that just sending off an e-mail does not get it beyond your PC. It is still sitting in your electronic out-tray until you dial up. More subtly, it is particularly easy to offend the recipient using an e-mail. On the phone or face-to-face your tone of voice and body language modify the message of the words. Letters have a certain formality that generally defuse any emotion. But an e-mail, quickly typed and sent, can portray unwanted feelings. One answer to this is to use the emoticons and contractions referred to in the section on the Internet (see page 111), but these methods don't sit well in a business context. The only real answer is to reread each e-mail before you send it. This need not take long, but try to take an outside view and spot anything that could cause offence. In the end, toning it down might reduce its impact but is more likely to get it taken seriously.

E-mailing a dinosaur

Large companies can hamper the advantages of e-mail. Because of (probably excessive) concerns about the receipt of dangerous items (see 'Safe e-mail' below), corporations sometimes restrict access to the outside world, keeping e-mail to an internal function. This greatly reduces the value of e-mail, whether you are inside the company trying to get out, or on the outside trying to communicate in. Sometimes also the quality of connection to the Internet for external connection is limited. This tends to occur where the company has a background of large, mainframe computers and uses old-technology e-mail.

The most significant risk to the value of e-mail is when the e-mail culture has not prevailed in a company. If senior executives don't handle their own e-mail, if large areas of the company don't have access to e-mail, if it would be frowned on to e-mail someone senior to yourself, the chances are that e-mail is not the communicating force it should be in the company. The importance of having the right culture is that a large company is unlikely to be sympathetic to those with their own portfolio, inside or outside the company, without such an approach. For example, the Fujitsu-owned UK computer firm ICL encourages staff for whom it is appropriate to work remotely. I spoke to John Ruscoe, who performs his job for ICL from a sheep farm in the Orkneys. He was absolutely certain of the need for the e-mail culture: 'I have access to everyone in ICL by e-mail. It's considered my right to mail the chief executive if I need to – and to get a reply. That mutual respect is what's needed more than anything else.'

NOTE . . .

One of the effects of e-mailing dinosaurs is that their systems may not be able to cope with properly handling attachments of documents. You may find that your documents arrive there (or documents come to you) as a long e-mail message with page after page of nonsense characters. The long-term fix is to get them to improve their e-mail. The short-term fix is to use one of the many software packages that can convert this garbled text into a file. Look out for UUENCODE, MIME Encryption and MIME-64 – these are the formats that are most likely to be mishandled by corporate e-mail.

Safe e-mail

Using e-mail, and for that matter any electronic information source such as the World Wide Web, has an element of risk attached. It is possible to use these mechanisms to distribute a virus. A lot of rubbish has been written about computer viruses, probably not helped by films like *Independence Day*, showing them to be weapons that are capable of defeating an alien attack. Computer viruses are programs like any other. They have to be run to do something. Once they have been run, they can hide themselves in such a way that they can run themselves again, and distribute themselves to other computers. They can also carry a payload, performing anything from silly tricks like putting up a funny message, to malicious acts like wiping a hard disk.

Computer viruses are a danger, but the risk is greatly exaggerated, and certainly is not a reason for ignoring e-mail and the Web. You can't get a virus simply by reading an e-mail message for instance – you would have to run a program sent with the message to get the virus. There is a more confusing style of virus, which seems to contradict this. It is possible for a document produced in a popular word processor software such as Microsoft Word to carry a virus. In fact such viruses are now the most common type. This seems to contradict the suggestion that you can't get a virus by reading an e-mail, but there is a difference. Word processors like Word are now so sophisticated that it is possible to write whole programs using the built-in macro features. Macros are provided to automate repetitive tasks, usually by recording what you do and playing it back, but it is also possible to write a virus this way.

So what can the chameleon manager do? You can't ignore e-mail – it's too valuable – but equally you don't want a virus. Word processor viruses are quite common in large companies and you will inevitably be exchanging documents via e-mail, making it easy to pick up a virus. At its simplest, you can tell modern word processors to warn you about macros in a document before running them. This is a bare minimum, but it would be a very effective investment to buy one of the cheap but powerful virus scanners available on the market. These run on your PC, watching out for infected documents and programs. See the Chameleon Manager Web site (http://www.cul.co.uk/chameleon) for recommendations of anti-virus software.

The unwanted virus

I recently received an e-mail from a corporate client which had a Microsoft Word document attached. As I saved it on to my PC, the bells and whistles went off on my virus detector. As it happened this was a relatively harmless Word virus which merely removed a few items from the Word menus and reproduced itself. The first lesson from the experience was the need to have a virus monitor even if you don't download software from dubious sources. The second was mild surprise that my virus checker – one of those 'generally never seen' facilities like anti-lock brakes or an airbag in a car – actually worked. But the biggest lesson came when I called the person who originated the document and pointed it out. 'It's all right,' he said, I've had my machine cleaned up since then.' It hadn't occurred to him that he had sent the document (and the virus) on to six other people. And it was left to me to make sure everyone else knew. This not uncommon attitude makes it pretty clear how viruses like this spread and thrive.

When to use what

With a range of communication facilities at your fingertips, there is sometimes some confusion over which to use in a particular circumstance. If face-to-face communication isn't an option, the phone remains the first choice for immediacy. It also has the advantage over the other technological means of being a direct interaction. Should there be need for clarification, it will give the fastest result. E-mail is now generally the choice should immediacy not be required. E-mail has immediacy from your end in that you can fire one off as soon as you have established the need to communicate. E-mail is also a very broad means of communication in that it can include documents and other computer files as attachments. E-mails can also be sent quickly, cheaply and efficiently to a large number of correspondents at once. And they have worldwide scope with a local call connection.

The fax might be losing its value, but it is still the easiest way of sending existing paper documents elsewhere immediately. You should think twice before sending unsolicited faxes. Not only can you irritate the caller by the timing (especially if you accidentally ring a voice line in the middle of the night), but receiving a fax has a significant cost in used paper. The post (snail mail, as it is derisively referred to by e-mail devotees) is only required now where formal or prestige communications, or physical objects are required. Typical examples of where the post may still be employed are sending brochures or invoices (though increasingly these are accepted via e-mail).

What can go wrong?

Communication is a very natural, seemingly very easy thing, yet so often it goes wrong. It seems as if through laziness or ignorance we mostly manage to mess up on communication. There are a number of ways that communication can fail which apply equally to large organizations or individuals. It is useful to look at the possible causes of failure to be on your guard. The barriers to communication listed below are from *Organisational Behaviour* by Roger Bennett (Pitman, 1997), though the interpretations are my own.

Message distortion

This is the classic communication problem where a message becomes modified or even lost as it passes down a chain. Be aware of the route your messages are likely to pass through in getting to important recipients. Is there any way to access those recipients at the end of a chain directly?

Information overload

It is very easy to receive so much information that important messages get lost. This often happens in a large organization that floods individuals with information or worse, useless data. As a freelance journalist I receive at least a dozen press releases a day, mostly telling me things I'm not interested in like 'Fred Smith becomes chairman of Lectro Corporation', or 'Nudger Networks introduces new Internet rerouter box'. The electronic age makes overload even more likely, as it is as easy to send an e-mail to 1,000 people as it is to one.

There is a range of tools available to help with overload. Where you are responsible for sending out data, take a leaf out of the book of Brian Thomas, Finance Director of financial services corporate Allied Dunbar. Thomas insists that any report, even a monthly expenses report, has recommended actions attached, banning sheets of meaningless numbers. Think twice before distributing something just for the sake of it. Attach a mental cost to the reading time. Incoming electronic information can now be filtered to some extent by software but, whatever the source, you will need to develop a scanning technique to pick up relevant information quickly. If you want to cut through someone else's information overload, the more personal the contact the better. The scale is roughly form letter, personal letter, fax, e-mail, phone call, face-to-face. Bear in mind, though, that without secondary support like recording, the low-presence methods (letters and faxes) are generally those which leave most trace if it is necessary to prove that you did something.

It is generally better to deal by speech than by letter.
(Francis Bacon, sixteenth-century philosopher)

Suitability of messages for a particular audience

General messages rarely work. You need to tailor your message to your audience. This is particularly easy to forget when communicating to a non-technical audience a technical subject which you are very familiar with. I appeared on *Watchdog*, a television consumer programme, talking about a computer product. As a journalist, I attempted to match my message to the audience, keeping out any reference to technical terms. But it was fascinating to watch an enthusiastic user of the product. Try as he might, all sorts of jargon kept slipping in. To succeed here you need to have a reasonable idea who your recipients are, and what their level of knowledge and experience is.

Semantic imprecision

Vagueness and ambiguity are easy ways to confuse or dilute the message. A natural inclination to caution may insert many qualifiers into your communications that make them seem uncertain and hence low in value. Compare 'it seems to me that the car probably has some functional mismatches or operational inconsistencies' and 'the car has faults'. There is the danger that the second statement will seem arrogant, but it conveys a lot more weight than the first. Even more dangerous is communication where it is not clear what you require. Improving your use of English can help, but you can't beat bouncing your communications off someone else and checking that they are hearing what you think you are saying.

Lack of opportunities for communicating

Communication can fail because it simply isn't possible to get through. At the end of last year I gave a series of creativity seminars for a UK corporation. I then had to obtain payment from them. To do this I had to communicate to three separate individuals – the training sponsor, someone in the purchase ledger department and someone in the purchasing department. Each rarely answered their phones, using voice mails. Each rarely returned calls. When I did manage to get through to one individual, they claimed they were having equal difficulties contacting the others. Apart from finding alternative routes, the main weapon here is sheer repetition. By repeatedly calling it is usually possible to find a crack in the communications barrier.

Inability to listen

Communication is about listening as much as it is about transmitting. What's more, you are more likely to be listened to if you are known to be a good listener. If listening doesn't come naturally to you, this is a really hard one to crack. There is no magic solution – just more listening. To begin with, watch yourself. When you find you are about to interrupt or cut across, hold yourself back. Listening takes a lot of development; don't expect overnight results.

Membership of a reference group

Everyone belongs to certain groupings: the family, neighbours, your work group, your social class, your political party, your religion, your ethnic origin etc. If the message is adverse to one of your so-called reference groups, you are likely to ignore it, or at least to water it down. Make sure that as much as possible you are aware of significant reference groups among your recipients and react accordingly. For instance, when communicating with a firm in Utah, it's not a good move to make jokes about Mormons.

Boredom factor

This is a category I have added. One of the biggest barriers to communicating is being boring. Academic sources are particularly prone to this. It's almost as if, in an attempt to appear scrupulously objective, they go out of their way to be dull. Yet there are plenty of great academics who have proved this to be unnecessary. You only have to listen to one of the recorded lectures of the great physicist Richard Feynman. Even if you don't understand the physics, it's hard not to be won over by the enthusiasm. Yet a great deal of communication, spoken and written, seems to imply that the communicator has no interest in the topic, and even less interest in being heard. Energy, good writing style and avoiding unnecessary complication can all help overcome the boredom factor.

Failed communications

Think back over the last few weeks. Try to pick out the best and worst examples of written and spoken communication you came across.

Step 1   *Thinking of the bad examples, which of the above failings were present? Were there any others?*

Step 2   *Thinking of the good examples, what made them good? What made them stand out from everything else you had read and listened to in the period?*

Step 3   *Next time you have to write a report or a proposal or next time you have to give a presentation or put across a message to a group of people, pause before delivery. Look back at the positive and negative lessons you've learned. How do you rate your own communication against these yardsticks? Are there any changes you can make before delivery?*

Step 4   *After delivery, check again. If there is any way of obtaining impartial feedback from the recipients, get it. How do you feel it went? How could you have done better?*

Result   *By comparing your own communication against these examples you should be able to improve. Everyone has gaps in their communication skills. As a chameleon manager, communications are vital to your progress. You can't afford to be second rate. Work on it.*

Quality communication

With so much to get in the way of communication, you need to concentrate on quality. However much we accept that 'the medium is the message', just as much importance attaches to the quality of the content as to the quality of the medium. It's true that a good message, poorly transmitted is likely to be ignored but, equally, a poor message with glossy trappings will soon be seen through and criticized. As a chameleon manager you will have to be a good communicator in every sense of the word.

Communication varies between the written, the verbal and the non-verbal. Most business writing is appalling. This isn't a criticism of handwriting – thanks to the word processor, actually reading the words isn't a problem, but absorbing the content is. Even business books are often stodgy and unreadable, let alone the typical memo or minutes of a meeting. The most frequent mistakes are trying to achieve a scientific detachment, and not reading a document through someone else's eyes.

As we have already seen, scientific communications tend to be sterile and clumsily written. The intention is to put across an air of objectivity; the effect is to make the fascinating boring. As management rather grandly considers itself a science, it seems that the same fallacy of mistakenly confusing objectivity and tedium has entered the sphere of business writing. To keep business documents readable, minimize unnecessary jargon. Jargon has its place as a shorthand, but shouldn't be used for its own sake. Keep documents short. Traditionally, the fatter a report, the more value it was considered to have. Aim for a one-page default length of any written communication. Never use long words simply to sound impressive. And avoid forced use of third party and indirect language. Don't say 'the project having been considered for advancement, it was cancelled due to counter-considerations in the steering committee', just say 'the steering committee cancelled the project'. Don't be afraid of 'we' or 'I'. If you are taking an action or making a decision, say so.

Never send out a document without reading it through as if you weren't the person who wrote it. This needn't take long, but it can be very valuable, and judging by the documents I see, few people actually do it. Look for typing mistakes (spelling is important, whatever trendy academics may say – it makes an impression). Ruthlessly weed out unnecessary redundancy. (Yes, I know. The previous sentence has a problem in this respect – if you can spot the deliberate mistake, you are well on your way to improving your own writing.) I regularly write articles twice the length required and manage to hack out half the words without changing the meaning. Try to give the document a structure that flows well. This can mean sensible use of paragraphs and sections. Also look for anything that stops it reading well (try reading it aloud). It's hard to turn out a masterpiece, but it's easy to change a nightmare into solid workmanship.

A quality document is more than just well-written words, it should look appealing too. Flip through professionally produced documents and magazines. Consider how your documents are different. If you are using a plain, typewriter-style font, it's time you crawled into the twentieth century and used something more attractive and readable. A broad rule (though like all rules made to be broken) is that a serif font like Times Roman reads better on paper, while a sans serif font like Arial reads better on the screen. Consider layout – it doesn't take anything spectacular to lift a document well above the common herd. Does it matter? Again, think yourself into the shoes of the recipient. No one is suggesting that a business proposal is going to be accepted simply because it looks good, but there's no doubt that it will have the edge over a tatty presentation which otherwise has similar merits. From simple observation of comments of would-be buyers, it would seem that many business cases and proposals are poorly presented. Why not give yourself the advantage?

Check your quality

Step 1   *Find the last three documents other than straightforward letters and memos that you produced.*

Step 2   *Look at them as a whole, without trying to read them. What does the appearance of the document, the way it is set out, say to you?*

Step 3   *It's hard, but try to look through the documents as if you've never seen them before. How easy is it to find your way around? Are they a comfortable read?*

Step 4   *With your documents alongside you, look at a few modern business books (including this one). Compare how the book lays out text with that of your documents. Why and how is it different from your style?*

Result   *This exercise isn't supposed to make you want to produce documents that look like a book. But next time you produce a report or a proposal, you can incorporate some of the ideas you've seen and pick up on some of the criticism you have made of your own documents.*

Speech and body

Quality in speech is harder to achieve. Preparation and appropriate notes are valuable for anything from an important phone call to a presentation to a thousand people – though in both cases reading from a script seems false and is best avoided. Keyword notes which remind you of the points that need to be made but don't force you into a particular set of words are best. You may be forced into using an autocue for legal reasons – otherwise avoid them.

Rehearse, but don't be rigid – if circumstances force your presentation or conversation in a direction you didn't expect, go with the flow.

There was a time when regional accents were considered a drop in quality. Now, if anything, they are a bonus. Speaking English with, for example, a highland Scottish accent or a French accent can be a positive asset. But do remember that, while an accent is fine, it becomes a liability if it gets in the way of comprehension. If you have a strong accent you need to revisit your dream portfolio and see if keeping your accent at its current strength is more important than achieving your goals. If it's not, look at ways of changing it.

Bear in mind also your non-verbal communication. A shallow understanding of body language is now very common, so you need to make conscious adjustments to what your body is saying if necessary. For instance, job interviewers will almost always know the basics of body language. If you sit with your arms folded or your hands linked it will be interpreted as discomfort. Make sure that you sit in a nice open position to show how positive and relaxed you are. It seems a con, but it serves them right for putting so much trust in such a widely known mechanism. Because body language is a natural inclination, you need to keep a constant mental eye on yours when in face-to-face communication. If you don't, it will betray you.

Communication overcoming management

key concept

Build and use your network.
You need e-mail.
Quality is essential in good communication.

Communications are of fundamental importance to the chameleon manager. There is hardly any aspect of a chameleon manager's job which is not dependent on the quality of communication. Working in a DisOrganized fashion, the chameleon manager needs to communicate to find new tasks, make the tasks happen, come to a close and carry forward to new work. Technology has a powerful role to play in this, supporting the network of associations that will be the backbone of communication.

In the next chapter we will see how part of the chameleon manager's job is to dispose of management, to move beyond management. It is only with superb communications that such a move is possible.

9 Managing without management

 key concept Total management skills, managing more with less.

Preview

- Traditional management skills were designed for a different era.
- Stability, production line ideals and direction have become change, individuality and leadership.
- Traditional compromise positioning between task and people focus, control and empowerment, innovation and responsiveness have to be replaced by extremes.
- Leadership takes over from management, replacing control and rules with direction and principles.
- Taking the management out of project management.
- Risk assessment is important, but keep it simple and involve the customer.

The skills of yesteryear

The frightening thing about becoming a manager is that you are suddenly placed in a position of authority without being any different on the inside. The good news is that a set of management skills have been assembled over the years to provide the tool kit for a good manager. The bad news is that most of these skills are either totally useless for the current business climate or at the very least in need of serious overhaul. The techniques and approaches still being taught were devised for a different era, when change was slower, information technology did not exist and a job for life was not a joke.

The position isn't entirely negative. There is plenty that can be retained from the old skills, but the chameleon manager needs to be prepared to abandon whole sections of received wisdom – particularly hard if you have been doing the same thing for many years – and take on new requirements.

Of course, there has always been a need for differing styles of management. In *DisOrganization* (see page 118), we specify business direction on four dimensions. These are management to leadership, task to people, reaction to innovation and centralization to fragmentation. In a similar way, an individual's management style can be broadly defined by the way they position between a focus on task and a focus on people, between control and empowerment, between reaction to demand and innovation. This is management as we know it.

MORE INFO . . .

For more on the way project management skills are changing, see *Strategic Skills for Team Leaders and Line Managers* by Michael Colenso (Butterworth-Heinemann, 1998).

A different requirement

In becoming a chameleon manager, it is necessary to throw off the fixed nature of management. In this sense, a chameleon manager really is managing without management. Just as in *DisOrganization* we suggest that a successful business of the future will occupy both extremes of each dimension at once, so a chameleon manager can't occupy a weak, fuzzy position somewhere in the middle of each spectrum. Instead they need to excel at both task and people orientation, at control and empowerment, at reaction and innovation.

A particularly worrying fact for the experienced manager is that many of the new skills are associated with youth. It seems at first that a new focus on individuality, a love of change and the seeing the merits of empowerment rather than traditional control don't sit well on older shoulders. Though there may seem to be some reassurance in the fact that both ends of the spectrum are required, it is certainly true that a chameleon manager needs more flexibility than a traditional manager. Moving quickly is essential. But provided experienced managers are prepared to learn, they will not be disadvantaged. Younger managers may find the business of change more exciting and less threatening, yet flexibility is often associated with the right kind of maturity and experience. If your attitude is 'I've seen it all before', you've got real problems. If it is 'there's always something new (thank goodness)', you're one step ahead of the newcomers.

Young men are fitter to invent than to judge, fitter for execution than for council, and fitter for new projects than for settled business. (Francis Bacon, sixteenth-century philosopher)

The portfolio-driven manager

One of the paradoxes of adopting a personal portfolio is that you begin to lose the traditional characteristics of a manager. Chances are, as a chameleon manager you will be less interested in company politics, because your focus goes far beyond the company. You certainly won't be a company person, bought and paid for. Whatever the outcome of developing your personal portfolio, though, you are still potentially a manager. If you move to self-employment, you will be manager of your own time. Whether or not you play a management role for your clients depends on the way your portfolio develops. Many senior managers who have spent years fighting the system heave a sigh of relief when the burden of classical management drops from them and they become a consultant or a contractor, but as such you should always remember your management responsibility to your own enterprise.

Task or people?

Traditional management focused on task. The whole ethos of the production line is task-centred. This approach led to the bizarre extremes of time and motion, where attempts were made to fit the people to the task, shaving seconds off here and millimetres off there with the intention of maximizing efficiency. Unfortunately there was a huge flaw in this approach. Even if you aren't interested in making employment fulfilling for your staff (and if you aren't you will never get the best quality staff, delivering the best results), the total task focus introduces a huge inefficiency into the process which more than compensates for any savings that time and motion studies can deliver. People differ.

This is so obviously true that it needs stating again. People differ. By treating people as interchangeable components, the old school of management was simply asking for trouble. If you really are interested in increasing productivity and efficiency you need to work to individuals' strengths, not to some hypothetical standard. What is more, by putting people first and building the processes around them, rather than fitting the people around the processes, you can not only increase efficiency but give the workers greater involvement, making them more interested in the success of a business. With hindsight, it is hardly surprising that someone building a car will take more pride in it if they are involved in the construction of a whole car rather than a single cog wheel on a production line. A similar argument stretches well beyond the conventional factory environment. Whether you are in the entertainment business or running a supermarket, everyone will gain from broadening the involvement of individuals.

It is interesting that, in an interview on the subject of organization, Brian Thomas, Financial Director of Allied Dunbar, commented that it was a disaster to try to fit people to an organizational structure. You had to build the organization around the people. If a financial services organization, hardly the most people-oriented sector, can take this approach, it is likely to have even more impact in other businesses.

But, of course, this is old hat, isn't it? People orientation has been around since the 1980s. Haven't practically all large organizations got mission statements with remarks about 'our people being our most important asset'? Well, yes, but how many of them actually walk the talk? When it comes to the crunch, when times are tight, which assets go to the wall first? Obviously not the most important ones. Presumably you will sell off your overpriced headquarters buildings, get rid of your executives' cars and so forth before sacrificing your most important asset? Presumably you will also pause in this endeavour to watch pigs flying past the executive boardroom window.

It sounds so far as if, rather than advocating both ends of the spectrum, task and people, that I am advocating a total concentration on people. If only it were that simple. The people side needs stressing because, despite all the fine words, most companies are still weak on people management. However, the task cannot be ignored either. Once you get on to the people bandwagon, it is easy to think that all you need to do is treat your people right and everything will work. In fact it is quite possible to love your people into the collapse of the company.

If there is a secret to managing both ends of this spectrum, it is a matter of proportion. As a chameleon manager, your task focus has to be very clear, and very simple. If, for example, you have a top ten concerns for the week, and your staff are well aware of what these concerns are (we aren't talking about just a printed list here, you need to talk about them), you have a better task focus than 99 per cent of managers. Does ten not sound enough? After all, as a busy manager, you have responsibility for hundreds of things. Of course you do, and most of them will (or could) happen without your involvement. In fact they'll probably happen better without your involvement. It really should not be difficult to have a maximum of ten priority concerns. Of course each one may break down into more detail, but that is not the problem.

With a close focus on these tasks, you can then bring in the people end of the spectrum. By sharing your priorities and concerns with your staff, you should be able to spend most of your efforts on the people, developing them to make sure that your requirements are fulfilled. The combination of a real people-driven approach with a clear, regularly updated task structure is a winning one.

Top ten

Step 1 *List everything that is important to you for the next week. Everything you need to do, people who are important to get in touch with and so on.*

Step 2 *Now identify the priority items. You may require two passes, one to separate those which must be done in the next week, a second to pick out those of maximum impact. If after the second pass you've still got more than ten, be ruthless. Knock off the least significant. If you've less than ten, reinstate the most important that aren't actually required in the next week.*

Result *The resultant list should identify your priorities. Just because some activities aren't on the list doesn't mean that they won't get done, just that they must take second place to your top ten. It can be very helpful to spend five minutes at the start or end of each week, identifying your upcoming top ten. As a final part of the exercise, you might like to think whether there are other people (your staff, your team, your partners) for whom it would be useful to know your top ten? If you work alone, this is less likely, but there still may be external partners who it can be useful to share this information with.*

Control or empowerment?

All this wishy-washy people stuff is all very well, but you can't show weakness, or they'll take you for everything you've got. Sound familiar? Far too much management has been about monitoring input – attendance, breaks, being at the workstation – with excessive zeal. This is crazy. It implies that what the staff are doing doesn't matter, as long as they are doing something, and that they can't be trusted. Who hired these people? Who went out and had a choice of all those bright-eyed, excited, dedicated new recruits, and managed to pick the idle swines who can't be trusted? It's worrying, isn't it?

So, is the solution to swing to the other extreme? Do we abdicate all control and let the staff sort themselves out? Empowerment is a fancy (and rather ugly) word – is it really the answer? In a word, partly. (Charles Handy argues we ought to say 'subsidiarity' instead, because 'empowerment' implies that the power originates centrally. I'm not sure this is helpful as, on the whole, the power in question, rightly or wrongly, has been held centrally in the past. Anyway, subsidiarity is just as ugly, and is much too reminiscent of the European Union.) It is necessary to give the employees the ability to make decisions on the ground. The manager usually isn't at the right place at the right time. Managing without management is about making sure that the people who are there, the staff, can take appropriate action without someone breathing down their necks. This implies trust, and it implies providing staff with enough information, freedom (and if necessary education) to do the right thing.

Remember, though, the 'both extremes' pledge. What happens to control in this picture? What happens is that control moves from input to output. To manage without management you will need strict controls on the output, while giving the staff much more freedom in how they achieve it. It's not surprising that I should advocate this – it's exactly what a chameleon manager is looking for in making their portfolio. And chameleon management is for everyone, not just the manager.

The biggest difficulty with measuring output is that the manager has to know more about the business. Any fool can measure inputs – you need to understand sausages (or software or holiday products) to measure outputs. Once more we see the need for expertise looming. An old-fashioned manager could get away without any real expertise in the business area. A chameleon manager can't afford this luxury.

Innovation or reaction?

This is the spectrum where there has always been some recognition of the need for a broader view. The traditional manager was required to react to the needs of his customers or clients, but also to spot where it was necessary to act without prompting. No change required for once? Not entirely. The normal approach was to use only a small part of the spectrum. You did what your customer wanted, as long as it didn't involve something you thought was unimportant. You acted, but only if something was likely to be broken if you didn't.

The chameleon manager has to push out the boundaries on this dimension, providing more innovation and more reaction. The extra impetus on innovation is a reference back to the sigmoid curve in Chapter 1. You need to fix things before they're broken. To manage appropriately in rapid change and frantic competition, you need to be looking for ways to make things better all the time. Use of the creativity techniques we covered in Chapter 5 will be essential in doing this. Similarly, it isn't enough to nod in the direction of customer requirements. The classic approach to customers was to ask what they want, interpret it, build it to your interpretation and give it to them. This applied to practically any managed activity. Now you need to do more. There needs to be more direct customer involvement and feedback through the process. The communications skills covered in Chapter 8 will be necessary here.

Innovation and reaction are a classic combination. In theory opposites, in practice they have to work together. The customer is always right – at least when something has gone wrong. But don't expect the customer to tell you what they want that's new. You need to feed that in. After all, you are an expert, aren't you?

Innovation or reaction?

Step 1   *Consider the last major business project or activity (major in the sense of taking a considerable amount of time and effort), now completed, that you were involved in. Identify who the main players were. Be clear about who were the customers. This isn't always obvious, but there should be some somewhere. You aren't undertaking the activity just for fun.*

Step 2   *Break down the project or activity into stages. How was it initiated? How was it authorized? What preparations were made? And so forth. At each stage, identify the contribution of manager(s), staff and customers.*

Step 3   *For each stage, try to establish how much the manager(s) were involved in reacting, and how much in innovating.*

Result   *You should have an idea how, in this particular instance, reaction and innovation combined to get the job done. Should there have been more of either, or of both? Only you can say, but it is instructive to bring out into the open exactly what was happening.*

Kill compromise – embrace both extremes

He never wants anything in life but what's right and fair; only when you come to settle what's right and fair, it's everything that he wants and nothing that you want. And that's his idea of a compromise. (Thomas Hughes in *Tom Brown's Schooldays*)

Compromise is a natural inclination. Few of us find it easy to embrace both extremes simultaneously. The skill of the chameleon manager is in having the flexibility to be aware of your limitations; to identify where you sit and be prepared to shore up your weak areas with prompts. For example, if you are strongly task oriented, you should schedule regular events in your diary which are people oriented. Looking at individual's progress, their desires, their achievements, their future, rather than linking everything to the tasks in hand. In fact, your diary is probably your most effective weapon in achieving the extremes. It is natural to put off anything that doesn't come within your comfort zone. By forcing it into your diary or task list (insisting that it is not removed, and only rescheduling if you increase its priority), you are much more likely to make something happen.

Non-fuzzy leadership: managing without management

It is possible to identify one end of each spectrum (people orientation, empowerment, innovation) with leadership and the other (task focus, control, reaction) with management. Yet I would say that good leadership represents my extremist view of embracing both extremes, while management has traditionally provided the compromise position.

Given that definition, it is easier to understand why there is a lot more management than leadership around. Leadership requires a much broader scope than management. To be a leader you have to be thinking of directions, and as such to understand the environment surrounding the business requirement, not just the business process itself. Leadership also requires much more trust and self-confidence. Managers can't trust staff to do the job required and have concerns about being stabbed in the back at every opportunity. Leaders haven't time for such petty concerns.

The trouble is, it's a lot easier to check a list of actions in a mechanical fashion and reprimand someone for not doing particular things than it is to set directions, tutor and get a feel for progress. It's much easier to have rules than it is to have principles. The most depressing thing about management is how much it is focused on what is easy to do. The pragmatist might say this is only a matter of doing what is possible. Yet that's the slippery slope to disaster. It's like only taking costs into consideration rather than benefits when you are assessing possible actions. Usually costs are much easier to measure than benefits, so this is the easy way out. The trouble is that there's nothing to stop you accepting all the low-cost, low-return options and totally ignoring the much more lucrative medium-cost, high-return options.

If you intend to survive, and particularly if you intend to move your career in the direction of your desired portfolio, it can't be enough to do the easy thing. You need to take on leadership. Remember, this isn't just the 'soft' option of people, empowerment and innovation. You need to be aware of the key tasks and to monitor them. You need to control the minimum of essentials strictly and efficiently. You need to react to customer and staff requirements just as easily as you innovate.

Projects without management

This managing without management stuff is all very well, but what about large-scale projects? Project management is hardly a new skill – what the chameleon manager needs to do is to adapt to a new viewpoint. After all, traditional project management hardly has a perfect track record. It sometimes seems that most complex projects, particularly those involving anything creative like computer software or films, come in late and over budget.

In a fascinating assessment of what can go wrong with massive software projects, Robert L. Glass notes a number of causes for project failure. These include incorrectly specified objectives, bad planning and estimating, unfamiliar technology, inadequate project management and insufficient senior staff involvement. Glass concentrates more on what has gone wrong than remedies, but management of risk and issues feature highly on his assessment of what was missing.

MORE INFO . . .

See Robert L. Glass, *Software Runaways* (Prentice Hall, 1998).

If project management is to become something more, something that can overcome these seemingly inevitable problems, risk and issue management are essential. We'll look at those in a moment. There is, however, something else that is needed – handling projects without management. It seems that a large part of the problem stems from project managers becoming overwhelmed with the detail and losing sight of the big picture. Project management software does not help here. It encourages a view of calculating everything down to the last second, to the last nail, so that a project manager's job increasingly becomes one of a bean-counter, not a leader.

To be effective, the chameleon project manager has to rid himself or herself of the burden of detailed project management. The first step is to understand just how fragile all this data is. Remember where the term 'project' comes from. It means something which is projected into the future – an estimate, a prediction – or to put it bluntly, a guess. Project management is guesswork. If that sentence gives you trouble, think about it. Project management is not a science, it's guesswork – hopefully very good guesswork, but guesswork none the less.

Given this beginning, it seems rather fatuous to attempt to decide everything to the last tiny detail, and even more fatuous to then monitor progress at the micro level. Does this sound like a recipe for anarchy? That's not what project leadership (for want of a better term) is about. What it should be about is setting clear milestones, and keeping track of what is happening across the project. The project leader (who despite current terminology I see as someone superior to the project manager) should set the direction, establish milestones and monitor progress against them. It is not this person's role to handle project management to the level of fine detail. If this is really necessary, hire an administrator, because that's all this part of the project is.

A particular danger, identified in a number of Glass's failures, is project creep. Here all the forecasting is for a limited development, but as it gets under way it grows and grows. Again, the answer is not strict adherence to a detailed specification. Remember, it's a guess. It will be wrong. Sticking to the specification is like saying, 'I don't care what you really want, here's what you asked for in your ignorance, and this is what you are getting'. A much better approach is the growing practice of timeboxing. Instead of having a fixed list, requirements can be added and dropped, but the whole process has to be finished by a fixed timescale, so the customers have to prioritize their requirements. Should a high priority item take longer than expected, a low priority item will drop off the list. Most projects involve several staged timeboxes, each with a predetermined level of functionality.

Risk and issues

Things will go wrong. It's obvious, isn't it? So why do we generally assume that they won't? One of the problems with risk assessment is that in theory almost anything can go wrong, and you can't plan for every contingency. Still, bearing in mind the requirement for a broad view when we're looking at the future, it isn't so much of a problem. It doesn't take a huge exercise to ascertain the most likely risks, and to have a plan in place to cope with them.

Often the mistake that is made with risk assessment is that it is carried out with the wrong people. If you perform a risk assessment without the front-line people involved, the ones who have been there and seen what happens, you are doomed to failure. Getting input from those at the coalface is essential to any chance of success. Their input may have to be moderated. It's not unusual under pressure to develop an excessive view of the capacity for disaster. Risk assessment isn't about cynicism, but realism – a quite different proposition. From the risk assessment you should identify a number of key areas to monitor for signs that imply a risk is being fulfilled, and alternative paths with their own milestones and/ or timeboxes to cope with them.

However good your risk assessment is, though, you will get it wrong. (This is a good argument for not putting too much effort into risk assessment. Yes do it, because you will identify the obvious things, but something always slips through the net.) If you doubt this, you are not paying any attention to the real world. Any company which could achieve perfect risk assessment would be running the world.

Invisible IT risk

Even stunningly effective firms like Microsoft sometimes get it wrong. When, in 1994, Microsoft was planning an on-line system to bundle with its Windows 95 operating system, there was no question of the Internet being a threat to it. Yet within months of the launch it was clear that proprietary on-line systems of this sort were doomed. Similarly, IBM executives, running one of the most highly managed companies in the world, would have laughed in your face in 1980 if you had asked if personal computers, then practically toys, would provide any threat to their business. They simply didn't exist as a risk.

Given this lack of infallibility, risk assessment needs to be followed up by issue-handling. Traditional project management is not particularly good at this, because too much is set in stone, in detail, up front. Issue-handling implies spotting situations that arise which will disrupt the project but which have not been identified as a risk. An example of this might be an airline faced with the Gulf War. The Gulf War was in no one's plans – yet as soon as it began, it was obvious that it was going to have a major impact on performance. The big advantage the chameleon manager has is that the broad, simple plan is much easier to modify to fit the new environment than a traditional, detailed breakdown.

Risky business

Step 1   *Think forward to the next major activity that you expect to start. If there is nothing on the horizon, think about the one you most recently started. If you carried out a risk assessment, put it in front of you. If you didn't, spend five minutes listing what the most likely risks are, and what you could do to avoid or ameliorate them.*

Step 2   *Are there any risks to which the response is 'do nothing' or 'give up'? If there were, would you find this a problem?*

Step 3   *Discuss the risks with the customers (if you don't know who they are, identify them first). Do they have the same views as you on what are risks, priorities and possible actions?*

Result   *This exercise is designed to help understand more about the nature of risk assessment. Too often, if it is done at all, it is without sufficient consultation with the customer. Customer involvement is crucial if failure isn't to result in blame. It's easy to rely on the business equivalent of those signs you see saying 'the management accepts no responsibility for . . .'. The fact is, such signs don't defuse blame if something goes wrong. But a discussion with the customer, ending with positive acceptance of the risk is much more valuable.*

Too often, also, we find it difficult to have 'do nothing' or 'give up' responses. The fact is, in a number of cases the most effective action when a risk is encountered is to accept failure and restart on a different route.

MORE INFO . . .

For more on risk and project management, see *Project Skills* by Sam Elbeik and Mark Thomas (Butterworth-Heinemann, 1998).

What comes first?

Whether you are dealing with issues or timeboxing, you must prioritize. This can be a painful exercise. Priorities have to come from your customers, not from you. Yet you have a responsibility to make sure that the customer gets it right. All too often in the past, although not explicitly said, this has been a matter of the project manager wielding a big stick and saying: 'Step aside - you are being parochial. I have the global view and it's what I think that counts.' This isn't acceptable any more. Apart from anything else, the global view is breaking down. Companies are becoming more federalized, dividing into smaller functional units to obtain the small company benefits of innovation and speed. You can't have this minicompany approach without giving the unit the option to go its way, not follow 'the greater good of the company'.

Even if the centralist view were right, the new business model is much more customer driven - you need to see your boss and your internal clients as customers, and give them the right to do what they want with their money. This doesn't preclude advice, though. Whatever role the chameleon manager has, they are liable to be consultants. It is perfectly valid to advise on priorities based on your expertise. For example, you may well have technical knowledge that your client doesn't.

Sometimes the knowledge is held by the client, but they can't or won't prioritize. The line is 'everything is important; we want it all done'. The simplest tool in such circumstances is one touched on in Chapter 5. For each of the possible actions ask: 'What will happen if we do nothing? What will be the outcome for the company? Will it make any difference? If so, what?' This can be an extremely valuable exercise in deciding priority.

Teams beyond management

 key concept

Management concepts have changed radically.
Leadership is the new essential.
Keep it simple.

Managing doesn't go away as you develop your portfolio, but expands to take in the portfolio itself. However, the new manager cannot rely on the old conventions and has instead to operate at the extremes of the spectrum – task and people, control and empowerment, innovation and reaction. This extremist view can be seen as leadership, replacing the compromise that was management. If the new manager is to manage without management, the contribution of the team becomes ever more valuable. In the next chapter we look at team dynamics.

10 Team players

	Managing team dynamics.

Preview

- Organizations are flattening and becoming fragmented.
- Teams are now the main focus of management.
- Teams range from short-term and cross-functional, to ongoing work group.
- The impact of personality on team behaviour.
- Keeping teams running smoothly.
- The virtual team.
- Teams can still work if you don't like teamwork.

Organizational collapse

There was something comforting about the old, deep, hierarchical organizational tree. I can remember in one of my first jobs, a more experienced colleague who had a (something like) fifteen-level tree on the wall with himself at the bottom and God or the chairman (I can't remember which was higher up the tree) at the top. It might have made him feel small and insignificant, but he damned well knew his place, like the servant of old.

In fact, a deep organizational structure is reassuring both because it somehow feels more solid and unchanging, and also because a deep structure means relatively shallow steps. There are lots of levels to climb, so you have something readily attainable to aim for. If there are only three or four levels in a company, that first step seems very high. If, however, the promotion prospect is from sub-junior analyst (second class) to junior analyst (second class), it feels entirely achievable.

Like all the rest of the crutches of the old management style, however, the deep organization is dying out. Even where you are dealing with a dinosaur organization, structures are flatter than they used to be. Where a company has taken a more radical step, perhaps restructuring as a set of independent operating units, each unit is more like a small business, and may have a only couple of levels. This means that promotion prospects all but disappear. Many of the staff will have to face up to year after year at the same basic level. Instead, the opportunity is to move around, gaining experience in different roles in the wide, flat structure.

This is a situation where the chameleon manager comes into her or his own. An approach where broadening replaces climbing, or at least reduces the urge to climb, is an almost inevitable consequence of establishing your dream portfolio. If you have staff, you will need to make sure that they too are moving into chameleon management – otherwise they will become frustrated by their environment. Whether or not you have staff, though, the changes in organizations mean that there will be more and more focus on the team.

Never mind the organization charts, where do you feel to be in any organizations you are part of? How would you feel if you never had a 'more important position', but instead had an interesting series of positions, with enough salary to keep you happy?

The phoenix team

As organizations have changed, so has the nature of the team. I would categorize the team as a phoenix which has risen from the ashes of teams as we knew them. Suggest the word 'team' to the general public and ask them what they think of, and the image that will generally come to mind is a sporting team. A single dedicated body with a uniform purpose and direction. In fact, the sporting team is often used as an illustration in business, drawing parallels between sporting roles and business functions.

This is the aspect of the team that is least relevant to the new, phoenix team. Where the old sporting model has a single, directed focus, business teams are now parallel and democratic. Parallel because you are liable to be a member of many different teams simultaneously. Democratic because part of the requirement for the team is to draw on the strengths of all the individuals involved, and not to have a collection of automata following a single, central will. Of course you can argue that most sporting teams are like this anyway. Most sport is a part-time activity and the best teams rely on individual initiative, yet the model is generally based on a less flexible picture.

The team spectrum

Not only are teams different from the old sporting image, but they occupy a whole spectrum of types. Teams can be short term, brought together to address a single issue, or can have an ongoing remit with no end in sight. Similarly, teams can be a tight-knit working unit of people with the same types of knowledge – a traditional programming or sales team, for example – or cross-functional, bringing together very different experience to get the broadest view.

However teams are composed, the essential tool for making them work is the knowledge that a team is an assembly of people, not a collection of inanimate components. Images of well-oiled machines are not just misleading, they are destructive. No one is a cog. This should be stating the obvious, but judging by the widespread application of mechanical reward and assessment schemes and the attitude of many managers, it clearly hasn't sunk in. As such, all interpersonal reactions are significant. A team that works well socially has a much better chance of working well practically. There is a lot to be gained from putting effort into the team early on to build social comfort if it is to function well in the future.

Similarly, it is possible for a team's work to be badly damaged by problems between team members. It is tempting to think that everyone involved is professional, and it should be possible to paper over the cracks, at least until your important deadline is met. Say two of your key players have become worst enemies – surely it would be better to wait until a quiet time to sort things out? It's a recipe for disaster. Not only are quiet times a fiction, a 'sometime never' sort of postponement, you cannot overestimate the destructive impact of such a rift. Both team members will actively damage not only their own work, but that of those around them. Instead, at least one of the individuals should be found new responsibilities with almost indecent haste.

As a chameleon manager, you will need to give particular consideration to the teams you are part of. Going for a drink or lunch with other team members, whether the team is a solid reality with an office to prove it, or a virtual team that never normally meets, is of great benefit to team effectiveness.

Team roles

By definition, teams are made up of more than one person, each with their own characteristics and natural tendencies. We will be looking, in the next section, at the use of personality profiling to try to identify what those natural tendencies are, but first consider what roles are available. Meredith Belbin developed a range of team member roles back in the 1970s. Any particular team could have a different combination of these roles (there could even be a single individual fulfilling more than one role), and there is no evidence that a particular combination produces a better team performance, though it is arguable that a team which has everyone performing the same role might hit difficulties. These roles are described below.

The co-ordinator

Confident, mature and extrovert, a good listener but equally a good speaker, the co-ordinator is the natural chair or facilitator. The danger with the co-ordinator is that others may see them as people who flourish on the work of others, at the extreme a showy, manipulative parasite.

The team worker

A strong contributor, but not inclined to make decisions, happy to go along with the group. Can be seen as weak by some.

The specialist

An individual whose input is purely driven by their technical expertise. The important aspect of their role to them is the content; everything else is unimportant. Sometimes considered dangerously amoral, and often not brought into the decision-making process.

The plant

A very unfortunate term as the natural association would be a spy for management, the plant is in fact an idea powerhouse. Plants are intelligent and creative, but may well be very introvert. This doesn't mean, though, that they are quiet – they can be very vocal in defence of their ideas, but lack the social skills to put them across well. Terms like nerd and propeller head adequately show the negative feelings that plants can generate.

The shaper

In some ways, a shaper is a co-ordinator with their niceness and sense of balance surgically removed. The shaper has lots of drive and will push to make things happen, without much consideration for others. The shaper enjoys pressure and argument, and can seem very intolerant to those who don't.

The completer-finisher

Always driven to get through, the completer-finisher is a doer, not a delegator. They are very conscientious, but are likely to worry, and will be seen as overly fussy by some other types.

The implementer

The good news is that an implementer is a great person for taking someone else's ideas and turning them into reality. They are very practical, but also tend to adhere strictly to a plan once established. Because of this they can seem nit-picking and inflexible.

The monitor-evaluator

The professional critic and reviewer, excellent at finding fault with others' output, and good also at suggesting positive improvement. Not given to original ideas, though, and can be an irritant from the inclination to correct. They will often be seen as cold.

The resource investigator

Laid back and optimistic, the resource investigator doesn't suffer from 'not invented here'. They are great at trawling through others' work, finding the best and using it constructively. However, the resource investigator tends to work at a high level, so they are much more interested in starting things off than finishing them – by that time they are already looking for something new.

MORE INFO . . .

For more on Belbin's team roles see *Management Teams: Why they Succeed or Fail*, by R. Meredith Belbin (Butterworth-Heinemann, 1981).

Most people have some degree of preference for a particular role, but are capable of undertaking several of them. The value of the Belbin categories is not really in slotting individuals into it, so much as a checklist for success. When experiencing problems with a team, it is useful to cast an eye over the Belbin categories and consider: are we lacking in this role? Would it help to improve things if we had more (or less) of it? What can we do to make this happen?

Team roles

Step 1   *Look at each of the team roles. Which would you feel most comfortable with? Which would you feel least comfortable with? Rank the roles on a comfort spectrum.*

Step 2   *Consider the last few team activities you took part in. Remember, the team might be traditional or virtual. Which role or roles did you undertake? Where do they fit on your comfort spectrum?*

Step 3 *Look at the other members of the team. Could you identify their roles? Was there an obvious gap, a role that was required, but wasn't fulfilled?*

Result *This exercise explores recent team roles. There is no right or wrong answer – the only motive is to get a better understanding of how you have operated in a team, and to be more conscious in future of what is happening, particularly if things start to go wrong.*

Personality profiles: essential tools or horoscopes?

Assessing how a team will perform and helping it to perform better greatly depends on the sensitivity and experience of the team's leader. However, there are a number of well-established methods available to categorize team members into broad personality types, and from that to be able to predict how different team members will react to each other. If such techniques really work, they have a number of potential benefits. Although it is a ridiculous generalization to say that every team needs a range of types, most teams will benefit from having more than one. For example, a team that is engaged in innovative research will certainly need people who are open, innovative and flexible. But a team entirely composed of such people will probably never come to any conclusions. They will continually search out new and interesting ideas, and drop them for the next idea. Such a team could do with one member who is more focused on detail and regimented to pull them into line.

Once you have a team in place, knowledge of personality types is useful both for the leader and the individuals in the team. The leader can identify potential problems, and can make best use of team members' capabilities. For the individual, use of this knowledge is generally one of overcoming friction. In the example in the previous paragraph, the team of wacky innovators would find the more organized individual irritating. The latter would keep getting in the way of the fun stuff, talking about budgets and outcomes and deadlines. However, if the team knows about each other's personality profiles, it is surprisingly easy to overcome this resentment.

The potential, then, is impressive. But is the whole thing a fantasy? Personality profiling is generally based on the work of Carl Jung, though the consideration that there are distinct types of personality goes all the way back to Hippocrates whose concept of four temperament types (apathetic, irritable, melancholic and optimistic) dates back nearly two and half millennia. The problem with the approach is that it sounds worryingly like horoscopes. Everyone is slotted into a category, and gross generalizations are then made about their behaviour.

In fact, the similarity is misleading. Where horoscopes deduce behaviour from an unlikely coincidence, personality profiling is a self-fulfilling prophecy, because it is based on questions about behaviour. What is more, while astrology often seems to put absolute faith in how an individual will react, personality profiling merely describes typical behaviour, accepting that anyone can act outside their personality type. In fact it is sometimes valuable to encourage someone to do so, provided everyone concerned is aware that this will be a cause of stress.

There are a number of commercial systems for assessing personality types. One of the best known is the Myers Briggs Type Indicator, which is linked to Jung's four category pairs of introvert or extrovert, intuitive or sensing, thinking or feeling and judgemental or perceiving. In the UK, the Insights colour wheel from Dundee-based Insights International has achieved considerable popularity. Other tests include Catell's 16 PF test and the California inventory. Such tests usually involve a degree of expense and training, particularly for interpreting the results. Many large organizations will already have a psychologist or human resources specialist who can help with testing.

If you are dealing with your own portfolio, you will have less opportunity to use testing to establish personality types, but an awareness of likely causes of friction, and the ability to discuss what is happening in these terms can be extremely valuable even if a test has not been used.

Simple profiling

Whether or not you go to the extent of employing a commercial profiling approach like Myers Briggs or Insight, you can engage in some simple profiling activities either as an individual or a team. While these may not result in such accurate division of types, they will give some indication of the way individuals see each other and how they might interact. The first two steps should be undertaken individually. The remaining step should be taken together as a group if you are dealing with a team.

Step 1 (individual) *In each of the six tables that follow give marks out of ten. The bigger the number the more you agree with the statement.*

Set A

	Score (0 to 10)
1. I enjoy giving a presentation to 100 people.	
2. I like attending cocktail parties.	
3. I enjoy being interviewed.	
4. I like surfing the Web.	
5. I enjoy playing team sports.	
A TOTAL:	

Set B

	Score (0 to 10)
1. First impressions are very important.	
2. Intuition is a powerful force.	
3. Work should be fun.	
4. Organizations should be built around people.	
5. If it feels right, you should do it.	
B TOTAL:	

Set C

	Score (0 to 10)

1. When travelling, I always pack at the last minute.
2. I enjoy change.
3. I learn something new every day.
4. I like dealing with several different projects simultaneously.
5. Success is giving the customer what they really want.

C TOTAL:

Set D

	Score (0 to 10)

1. I don't like to rock the boat.
2. I keep a diary (or would like to).
3. I enjoy reading fiction.
4. I had my own fantasy world as a child.
5. I prefer a closed office to open plan.

D TOTAL:

Set E

	Score (0 to 10)

1. I find lists very useful.
2. Planning is often more enjoyable than doing.
3. I can't play a game without reading the rules first.
4. The country is going to pieces as we lose authority figures.
5. I usually arrange books alphabetically on the shelf.

E TOTAL:

Set F

	Score (0 to 10)

1. I can't see anything wrong with eating dead people.
2. I enjoy solving puzzles or crosswords.
3. I like to know how things work.
4. Paranormal happenings have normal explanations.
5. All feelings are reducible to chemical reactions.

F TOTAL:

For each table add up the total out of 50. Now move the totals into the boxes below and perform the simple calculations to obtain three scores out of 100.

A TOTAL:		F TOTAL:		C TOTAL:	
	+50		+50		+50
=		=		=	
− D TOTAL:	−	− B TOTAL:	−	− E TOTAL:	−
SCORE 1:		SCORE 2:		SCORE 3:	

Step 2 (individual) *Mark the positions of your scores on these scales by drawing a mark at the approximate position.*

Score 1

Internals | | Externals

| 0 | 50 | 100 |

Score 2

Feeling | | Logic

| 0 | 50 | 100 |

Score 3

Structured | | Flexible

| 0 | 50 | 100 |

TEAM PLAYERS

Step 3   *Compare the results on your chart with those of other members of your team. Look for differences and similarities. Where there are significant differences, be aware that there may be misunderstandings and discomfort with the others' approach. Where there are similarities be wary of the possibility of complacent acceptance of each other's faults.*

Result   *This is not a scientific assessment, but is (very) broadly based on conventional Jungian personality typing. The first chart looks at the importance to you of internal and external things. Traditionally referred to as introverts and extroverts, those individuals at the extremes will have very different approaches. The second chart considers how much you rely on logic and how much on feelings. The third compares your approach to flexibility and regimentation. There is no right or wrong. The point is, rather, to understand how different members of your team are liable to approach life so that you can give greater consideration to potential areas of friction and balance strengths.*

Oiling the mechanism

So you've got a team, and you've identified how individuals will work together – how then to get the maximum effort from the team? We've already got the Belbin categories as a first aid kit, but we need something more. After all, the best teams really do generate that unlikely concept, synergy, producing more than the sum of their individual efforts. Having said before that a team isn't a well-oiled machine, I have fallen into the trap of using the analogy of oiling the mechanism. In fact, because the team is an organic entity, it's more a matter of giving it a good diet, appropriate exercise and some fun. (This is a good example of why the machine analogy fails. Generally we don't think that a machine will work better if it has fun.)

In this organic analogy, feeding properly is about ensuring that the work that the team does is appropriate. Teams might be wonderful, but they aren't the best tool for every job. The old joke defines a camel as a horse designed by a committee. (We tend to forget that committees are teams. So do committees.) Much creative work is best done by having individuals generate a concept, then bouncing it off the rest of the team for improvement. Similarly, teams are often applied to tasks which simply don't need a group of people. The outcome is the same, but the effort applied is multiplied up by more than the number of people on the team. (More than, because the reverse of synergy happens and people get in each other's way.) A quick check that a task can't be equally effectively handled by an individual is always valuable before the team takes it on.

Keeping up the organic parallel, the best exercise is a regimen that stretches the individual. Similarly, a team can find ways of working that will improve its output. Probably the most important contribution is communications. Even if a team is located in the same office, but even more so if it is fragmented across a site, a country or the world, the need for good communications of who is doing what, by when (and why) are essential. Too often teams trip up due to misunderstanding, overlap and incompatibility. In the world of computer software there is a concept referred to as the API (application programming interface). The writer of one piece of software publishes an API. This allows other pieces of software to interact with the first program. The other writers don't need to know how the first piece of software works, just what the programming interface is. Similarly, team members don't need a complete knowledge of what everyone else is doing, but need well-defined interfaces.

A useful tool in improving the exercise routine of a team is Edward de Bono's Six Thinking Hats. De Bono categorizes the styles of input to a meeting or discussion into six different types, each assigned a coloured hat as an *aide-mémoire*. He suggests that by giving a discussion an explicit structure, it is possible to overcome the usual waste of effort on argument, where the whole business of winning and losing becomes more important than coming to the best conclusion. Instead, by using Six Thinking Hats, a structure is imposed that forces even the most pessimistic to look at the positive, and the most optimistic to consider what can go wrong.

TEAM PLAYERS

The Six Hats are:

- white for facts and information – getting the background data in place
- red for feelings – establishing a gut reaction without any basis on logic
- black for negative assessment – looking at the logical negatives of the discussion
- yellow for positive assessment – finding everything that is good about the point
- green for creative – looking for new, innovative approaches
- blue for overview – considering the process and the overall content.

By explicitly focusing on one of these modes at any one time, but also ensuring that the others are covered, a much more constructive approach can be established.

MORE INFO . . .

Edward de Bono provides a full discussion of using this approach in *Six Thinking Hats* (Penguin, 1987).

Finally, but equally importantly, comes the fun. I have already suggested that improving team socialization is a valuable way of improving teamworking. It also helps to establish a climate of fun within the team environment. If the team is office based, this can be through mechanisms like décor, toys and short on-the-spot social niceties. I have seen coffee and doughnut sessions, or just bringing Danish pastries to a team meeting be very effective at warming up the atmosphere. Whatever the basis, a light-hearted approach, humour and banter, and a lack of self-importance on the part of management can help. Where you have specific team-building meetings, fun can take many forms. I have run very effective team-building meetings in a team member's home (with lunch at the local pub), which almost inherently generates a more relaxed and fun atmosphere (provided it is done with the individual's enthusiastic consent).

Support for the supporters

Jean was running a support department. It was under pressure, but she felt that it was going quite well. It was a surprise, then, when one of the staff who she trusted came to her and said that there was a real problem, that the staff felt unwanted and that no one was interested in their views.

Jean could have reacted negatively, either denying the suggestions or taking it out on the staff. Instead she arranged for a day's team-building session at a management training centre. She set the broad programme to involve building a strategy for the department and dealing with the main issues, but left it to the staff to arrange the sessions. She participated, but as much as possible held back to become a contributor, not a manager.

The day was a great success. The staff felt that they were really contributing to their direction, and started acting as a team. A particularly strong feeling was that they were valued, because instead of using some cheap, in-house training room, Jean had used the smart management centre. It is quite often these small details which have most impact.

A healthy team

Next time you have a meeting with a team that you are involved with, think in advance of some way of bringing fun into the meeting. It might just be a social injection, like providing some interesting refreshment, or it might be a short fun activity as part of the agenda (hidden or announced). Even if you are working for yourself you will have virtual teams, working with other people who sponsor the work you do or are co-workers. Surprise them – do something to increase the health of your teamwork.

Having tried it as a one-off for this activity, consider ways of institutionalizing fun. The problem is that you can't fix it in concrete. To keep the fun alive, the approach has to be kept fresh. But there's nothing wrong with making it a fixture that something is done.

The company as a team

It is quite popular to extend the team concept to the company as a whole. This is all very well, but needs to be undertaken with care. If, as I have suggested, a team is very much a group of individuals with social interaction rather than a homogeneous mass, it is inevitably much easier to deal with a team which has a natural social sizing of five to ten, rather than a 'team' of 50,000, or even 500. Once it is impractical to know each team member personally the nature of the team is changed drastically for both the leader and the members.

One of the reasons that Paul Birch and I suggest that around the fifty mark is a good maximum size for the minicompanies we describe in *DisOrganization* (see page 118) is that seven is a good team size, so fifty (okay, forty-nine) is a team of teams. If a medium-sized or large company is to function as a team, it can only be effective by considering the team in the form of such groupings. This doesn't mean that it is impossible or even undesirable to set broad directions, principles and culture across a whole company. In fact, such an approach is necessary for success. But it is a mistake to think that doing so makes the company a team. These are attributes of a team, but they don't make a team – to think so is a bit like assuming that painting a car red turns it into a Ferrari.

The virtual team

It is possible to have teams that rarely if ever meet. As a chameleon manager, you are likely to be involved in such virtual teams on a regular basis. As a trivial example, the production of a book like this involves teamwork between the author and a range of individuals employed by the publishers, yet typically there will have only been one or two face-to-face meetings with the editor at the outset. Everything else is conducted remotely.

Such virtual teams do work well, but have limitations that you should be aware of. Without excellent communications they are prone to delay and misunderstanding.

AlphaBlox

High-technology software company, AlphaBlox, was established as a virtual team with offices in several continents. The idea was that, with the communications revolution that was the Internet, it should be possible to make the whole corporation virtual. However, within two years of setting up, AlphaBlox had coalesced on to a single site in Silicon Valley. Why? Chairman Michael Skok was very clear.

'In software, the US market is so dominant that if you don't claim an early market here, you don't get global success. Paradoxically, part of the reason that location is so important is the Internet explosion. It is all driven from Silicon Valley – even Boston is too far away. This ironic development in a business of instant communications is endemic to a technological industry where you are developing leading, or even bleeding edge products. You can't avoid the need for "face time". You can't do this sort of development with the asynchronous communications of e-mail or battling against time zones. The only efficient way to do it is face to face ... I can walk down the road here to many of our strategic partners. Others are a thirty-minute plane ride away, and in the same time zone. The really successful corporations will be those that form an ecosystem around them where their allies benefit from such partnerships.'

Skok was referring specifically to companies and partnerships, but there are some issues here for any virtual team.

In the AlphaBlox case study, the virtual team would not work, but for many chameleon managers they have to. In fact, of course, many of Skok's teams in the final organization are virtual, but the interface is face-to-face rather than electronic. It is certainly worth noting that it is impossible even for a high-technology company to overcome the benefits of direct social contact. Try to build opportunities to meet into your virtual teams.

TEAM PLAYERS

But I'm not a team player

Many of us are not natural team players. We like to work alone, to produce something that is identifiably ours. I've a suspicion, based only on very scant evidence that such behaviour is strongest in children without siblings. It also seems linked to the conventional ideas of creativity. While anyone can have their creativity improved by the sort of techniques covered in Chapter 5, it is certainly true that there are individuals with a stronger inclination to creativity. Such people, whether they become artists or painters or writers, or whether they have a more mundane job, are less likely to be enthusiastic team players than most.

This is a problem that could apply both to staff that you work with and to you yourself. The first step in dealing with the situation is to remove the unfortunate implication of the previous sentence. I have known people who have been very perturbed by their lack of team spirit. It's not surprising. The team ethos is hammered into us in school, in sporting activities and in the armed forces. It sounds terribly trite, but the first step of dealing with the non-team player is by changing it from a problem to an opportunity. To cease thinking 'how can we correct this fault' and start thinking 'how can we make use of this ability.'

There is nothing to stop the individualist making an excellent contribution to a team, it is just a different type of contribution, and may require a different type of team. Where, for example, two people working on a report together who were team players might develop the document sitting alongside each other, the individualist will want to go off and write a chunk alone, then swap the results with his or her collaborator. The outcome is not worse, just different.

Similarly, if you yourself are not a great team player it doesn't necessarily mean that you will be a bad team leader. In fact, many of the best leaders aren't good team players, because they will place the well-being of the team they run (but aren't really part of) above the well-being of their peers, i.e. the team they supposedly belong to. Without doubt, the chameleon manager needs to be able to work with teams at the drop of a hat, but it certainly isn't necessary to be a natural at teamwork and team dynamics.

Today the team, tomorrow the world

Teams will be important to you whatever you do.
An understanding of personality types will help team working.
Teams need feeding, exercise and fun.

The team is an essential unit of new business and new management, but it is a very different team to the old, dedicated sports analogy. It is not a machine, but a set of organic combinations, highly dependent on personal inter-action. As a chameleon manager you are liable to be part of many parallel teams, some virtual, some physical. The team is a great benefit, but be careful with it. Not only is it a dangerous picture to take too literally for a whole organiza-tion, it needs nurture. If a team is organic, you need to consider the aspects of nutrition – feeding it the right tasks, exercising it to ensure that the team works well together, and having fun.

Traditionally we have thought of teams within a company, but the need to consider group interaction goes even further. As Michael Skok of AlphaBlox observed, links with partners are just as important as any internal links. In the next chapter we will look at the way you will need to interact not only with your clients but with partners, competitors and others.

11 We are not alone

key concept	Managing network relationships.

Preview

- Managing without control.
- Managing outwards as well as inwards.
- Forming partnerships and alliances.
- Seeing the customer as another ally.
- Handling the competition.

Can you manage what you can't control?

In the traditional picture of management, the manager is in control. There is a rather quaint term sometimes used in the systems world that probably originates from the military – 'command and control'. The suggestion is that the manager sits at the centre of his or her empire, pulling the strings to make everything happen. Frankly, this has always been an unlikely picture. Even with machines, such absolute control is rare. Does this seem a strange statement? Surely you are in full control of a machine? Few PC users would agree. Too software dependent? How about motorists then? Even with the simplest of machines like a nutcracker, it is rare to be able to crack each nut easily without damaging the kernel. If we can't exercise control over such a simple thing as a machine, it is hardly surprising that control is something of a laughable concept when applied to a team or a business.

None the less, within a company you will at least have some instruments of control, however weak or faulty. You can hire and fire people (subject to restrictions). You can change suppliers (if there are alternatives). You can set directions or give orders (you may even have some obeyed). Management is at least a faintly logical concept within your company. But what about externals, the things which are outside our control? If modern business is all about partnerships, customer contact and dealing appropriately with competitors, how is it possible to manage these people who are totally beyond your control? For the chameleon manager the task is even more challenging, as the concept of 'internal' may well only extend to you as an individual. Everyone else is a supplier or a partner or a customer or a competitor, or most likely a combination of several of these.

It would be almost impossible to imagine exerting traditional management methods on many of these external entities. Yet management of a sort – not surprisingly chameleon management – is both possible and necessary.

MORE INFO . . .

Joanna Howard's *Managing More with Less* (Butterworth-Heinemann, 1998) expands on the theme of managing what you don't control.

Managing outwards

The art of managing outwards is a more delicate one than inward management. All you have to work on is influence. A prime illustration of influence is advertising. The advertiser can't order a customer to buy a product. Instead an attempt is being made to make the consumer aware of the benefits of a particular purchase, or even just to give the consumer a warm glow associated with the product.

All the categories of external management apply equally well to a company and to the individual chameleon manager. You will have suppliers, partnerships and alliances. You will have customers. You will have competitors. In managing these groups you will seek to influence the way that they deal with you. In the early stages of this book you were encouraged to set yourself a dream portfolio. External management is about influencing those who have the ability to help make your dream come true or (more likely) to prevent it from happening.

As you assess your externals, you are likely to find some that are totally unsusceptible to influence. Here you will have to consider what other actions you can take to mitigate or avoid these externals impacting your action. For example, the weather is a classic external that is not subject to influence (unless you have the resources to engage in weather control). If weather is likely to impact on your activities you will need to consider just what adverse weather can do to you – can it bring down power lines, can it rain off an outdoor activity, can it drown out quiet sound with wind noise or not provide snow when you are depending on it – and take action to provide alternative sources of power, a covered venue, a wind-proofed corner, fake snow or a different location.

Similarly the forces of law and government will have an impact, even though they are disinterested parties. In fact, they can comfortably be lumped in with weather, as they too are not open to influence (unless you resort to serious lobbying or bribery), but certainly can be mitigated. We won't be considering these disinterested externals much more. In most cases you will need to get professional help in dealing with them, in the form of a lawyer or an accountant.

Influencing without authority

There are times when the best example is one of how not to act. Phil was a superb example of how not to influence without authority. Phil had many of good ideas, plus the inevitable bad ones. The problem is, he had no authority to get his good ideas implemented. This needn't have been a problem, but for his attitude. First, Phil was a conspiracy theorist. Whenever things didn't go his way, he was convinced that there was an organized attempt to do him down. What he failed to realize was that, not only were senior management not really interested enough in him to put the effort in to make a conspiracy, but the chances are they couldn't have organized one if they had tried.

Secondly, Phil's interpersonal skills were weak. He was offhand and rude without meaning to be so. He demanded, rather than requested. He rarely complimented anyone on success, only ever criticized failure. Then he was surprised when there wasn't a rush to follow his star. If his colleagues were asked to liken him to a character in Winnie the Pooh, they would have uniformly chosen Eyore. Thirdly he lacked pragmatism and application. He was interested only in doing the absolute right thing. He didn't care if the result wouldn't be of any use. It wasn't utility, but theory that drove him.

Finally, he was dogged in entirely the wrong way. There is nothing wrong whatsoever with being dogged. Some of the world's greatest business people have got there through sheer determination. But the best sort of dogged person knows when to quit and start a different line — before everyone is heartily fed up. You don't get support from bored people, or those who comment under their breath 'here he goes again'. Phil never realized this. His influence remains very limited.

Who are they?

It is not possible to manage without knowing who or what you are managing. Much has already been made of your network and information sources. In building your network, in developing your information, you should have a good idea of what your external influences are, and some knowledge of their nature. Even so, it is worth explicitly noting them. Sometimes these external influences are known as stakeholders, but the term is too limiting for the considerations we have here. You certainly need to know who has a stake in your activity, but it is easy to overlook the competitor and the disinterested external that can still have an impact.

Step 1   *Consider the most significant project or activity you were engaged in last week. Without any concerns about categorization, spend a minute jotting down all the external influences on your activity.*

Step 2   *On a separate piece of paper, note down everyone who might be considered a supplier to your activity. Next note everyone who might be considered a customer, client or user. Next add any partnerships or alliances that may contribute. Now consider competitors. Are there any competitors who in any way influence your activity? Finally consider the disinterested externals. Are there any governmental, legal or natural conditions etc. which might be relevant?*

Step 3   *Compare the two sheets. Have you got anything extra on the second sheet? Is there anything on the first you didn't add under any of the categories? Is it because it doesn't fit – if so, what should the category be?*

Result   *Often you will add influences once you start to consider the various possibilities. It is always useful when considering what you need to do to make an activity succeed to run through all the influences (external and internal), being clear what you need to do about them.*

I want some now

Probably the most comfortable and familiar external relationship is with suppliers. This isn't to say that it is always easy, but a supplier generally feels more like an internal relationship than most. You can tell a supplier what it is that you want, and expect to reprimand them if they don't come up to scratch.

An important starting point in considering your suppliers is to ensure that you don't exclude anyone from the category because they aren't conventional suppliers of goods. A supplier isn't just someone you buy a physical item off. A supplier can be providing a service or an intangible product. A supplier can be internal to a firm you work for. Once you have identified who your suppliers are, many of them can be disposed of immediately – not because they aren't important, but because you need to turn them into something different. A supplier/purchaser relationship is very one sided. Traditionally there needs to be no communication beyond 'this is what I want' and 'this is what it will cost', with the supplier trying to provide as little as possible, and the purchaser trying to obtain the best price from the supplier.

The chameleon manager requires a very different relationship with suppliers. Where appropriate they need to be turned into partners. This recognizes a very important aspect of the business interaction. If your business model is to screw your customers you are likely to lose them to someone else or to bankrupt them. Similarly, if your attitude to suppliers is not to pay them if possible, and if paying becomes necessary to pay the minimum you possibly can, you are going out of your way to make it difficult to continue a working relationship. It's not that you need to be all soft and cuddly. In a partnership you can still be looking to get the best practical prices, but you can share the reasons why a particular price or timescale is impossible, or why it is essential to pull out all the stops and get something done ahead of schedule. The real difference between a partnership and a supplier/purchaser relationship is shared information and goals. If you can achieve this with your suppliers, you move the goalposts very effectively.

To read some management texts, however, (and I have to confess to having been guilty of this myself occasionally) you might think that all suppliers can be turned into partners. In reality, there are some supply relationships which either don't merit the establishment of partnership, or are impossible to move. If you want to buy a single box of paperclips which will last you for the next ten years, you are unlikely to develop a true partnership with your local office supplies store. Not only is the effort totally out of proportion with the reward, but the reaction of the counter staff to the proposal is likely to be incomprehension at best. However, if you are in the business, for example, of buying furniture for a large company, you have the opportunity to bring partnership into play.

As you build your portfolio, you are likely to be dealing with suppliers more and more on your own behalf. Most managers outside the purchasing profession are likely in such circumstances to give suppliers too much rope. This isn't a matter of being aggressive, but many of us are wary of even being assertive. Haggling is something market traders do, not business people. It feels embarrassing to ask if there is a discount, if there is some way a price can be brought down. Many of us find it quite difficult to question the price tag or the delivery schedule, but such discussions are not in themselves destructive, and many suppliers have regular discounts available which aren't applied automatically, but will always be provided if asked for.

A final consideration is whether the supplier is also a customer. If you are tempted to mistreat a supplier, make sure that they don't also buy from you. In fact, make sure they are never likely to buy from you. It is not unusual for a company, particularly a large company, to be heavy-handed with a supplier, only to discover that that same supplier takes three times as much business from the company as they supply. This is a particularly easy trap to fall into if the two businesses are very dissimilar. For example, airlines have been known to try to screw the last penny out of their toothpaste supplier, only to find that they are risking a large amount of business from a multi-national cosmetics firm in exchange for a few pounds saved on in-flight luxuries.

Partnerships and alliances

Government and co-operation are in all things the laws of life; anarchy and competition are the laws of death. (John Ruskin, nineteenth-century critic)

Partnerships and alliances are probably the most difficult of business relationships. How often have you seen news of such an example of business hand-holding, only to find that it has collapsed before any real benefits can be accrued? Similarly, in small business, the dangers of doing work for friends and relations can be all too real. The problem with both examples is the breadth of the partnership. An attempt is being made to marry up two very broad entities. There may appear to be strong similarities on the surface, but the more effort is put into the partnership, the more it becomes apparent that there are differences. These differences can whittle away trust and establish quite different directions which will eventually pull the partnership apart.

Partnerships succeed or fail on exactly the same grounds as personal friendships or marriages. It may seem excessive to apply such a fuzzy, illogical picture to the negotiations of two major businesses, but those involved in such negotiations always have stories of petty actions or trivial considerations that can halt progress. There have been business alliances which have collapsed over the name of a product, or the use of a colour. There have been major partnerships which have been undermined by the negative attitude of one member of the negotiating team. Inevitably, then, many of the skills of managing partnerships are interpersonal ones.

There are other considerations as well, though. Bear in mind the breadth problem. Breadth leads to difficulties of assumption – you can't cover everything and thus make incorrect assumptions, inevitably leading to conflict. By keeping the partnership very tight and focused, with clear ground rules, there is a much better chance of success. Does this mean having a legal document defining responsibilities and limitations each time you do anything in partnership? No. Of course legal documents are necessary for full business partnership, but there should not be a need for this approach if we are talking about a partnership like an improved supplier relationship or with another team in the same company. Internal contracting is fine as a way of making sure everyone understands what the desired outcomes are, but shouldn't be used as a stick to try to control a partnership. If there aren't individuals in the other party that you can deal with and trust, the partnership is bound to fail.

Cosseting the customer

Managing the customer should be a normal requirement of all business, yet so often we provide terrible customer service as if it was the natural way of things. In the UK our customers put up with surly staff and poor delivery. In the more demanding USA there is a veneer of good customer service, but much of it is artificial and inflexible. As a chameleon manager you will be dealing with customers at two levels. You will have your personal customers. They are the people directly commissioning and using your work. It doesn't matter what you do, whether you are a freelance artist, a salaried project manager or a director of a major concern, you have personal customers. You will generally also have second-level customers – the customers of the company you work for, your client's customers. Each level needs management.

We have already looked at the importance of customer information and maintaining a good relationship with your personal customers. This has to be the basis for management of this group. You don't have the same level of information about your second-level customers. You can, however, manage the relationship using a few simple tools. A good way to see how not to do this, and hence provide lessons for good practice, is using the horror story.

Customer service horror stories

Step 1   *Sit down and think back to your experiences of being a customer. Whether you were buying something in a shop, or employing an estate agent, pick out any horror stories you can recall. Note briefly what happened. Sadly, you should find no problem filling a page.*

Step 2   *Look at each horror story. What were your suppliers doing wrong? Why did things go wrong? What irritates you about the way that you were dealt with?*

Step 3   *Just so you don't feel too miserable, repeat Steps 1 and 2, but looking for delight stories. The sort of customer service you want to tell other people about. You will probably have fewer examples, but they should provide some clarity on what doing it right is all about.*

Result   *It is quite frightening how everyone can wheel out a collection of bad service horror stories. Hopefully you have some delight stories too. I am about to describe what I think causes things to go wrong (and right), but there is no better lesson than practical experience.*

WE ARE NOT ALONE

Customer action

What most customer relation problems seem to amount to are lack of information provided to the customer, lack of delivery on promises, lack of listening and apparent interest in the customer and lack of product knowledge. You can't order your customers to use you, or even to use you again after a first experience, but you can influence them by making sure these categories are covered.

When dealing with customers, try to anticipate the information that they are likely to need and have it ready. So often you hear a response which boils down to 'you don't need to know'. This is a customer management disaster. It either means that you don't know the answer, but are ashamed to say it, or that you consider the customer to be of inferior intelligence, hardly an attractive message. If you don't know the answer, the only acceptable approach is to say so, but to link it with a promise to find out. It's hard to do. Few of us like to admit to ignorance. But such honesty almost always gets a good reaction. If you do know the answer, it really isn't up to you to decide whether the customer needs to know. To tell the customer otherwise is suicidal.

If you promise to find out the answer to a question, it is essential then to come back to the customer. If you are likely to forget, find some mechanism (your diary, a task manager) to flag up the need to respond. While the promise is reassuring, it only takes a couple of instances of nothing happening for your reputation to be broken. I generally note action points in an electronic organizer. When I did this at a business meeting, a customer noted that when another of his suppliers made a note like this it was a sure sign that nothing would happen. I had to go out of my way to prove him wrong. Even if the response is to come back on a regular basis and say 'I don't know yet, but I'm still working on it', it makes so much difference to be the one to act. As soon as the customer has to ring you up to see what you are up to, you have lost. This is a specific example of delivering on a promise, but any customer interaction where you promise to do something by a date requires similar monitoring and feedback.

Listening is just as important as being proactive. It is very easy to listen to the minimum of what a customer says, then switch off and go into automatic pilot. You can see it time and again in retail interactions. You go into the shop or ring up the sales line and start to explain what you want. After the first sentence, the sales assistant stops listening, having made an assumption about what you want, and produces the entirely wrong object. Attitude and interest in what the customer is saying really does make a difference – and it isn't always about the obvious. Last year I twice had to take something to a supermarket customer service desk. The first, Sainsbury's, was an item I had accidentally taken through the checkout without paying for. The service agent was polite and complimentary that I had been so honest. The second, Tesco's, was to take back a £5 note I had found on the floor. The service agent made me feel I was wasting her time, and was mad for not pocketing it. Not only did it (probably unfairly) bias my attitude towards these two supermarkets, I was telling the story for months afterwards, influencing others as well.

Product knowledge is equally often a problem in retailing, with assistants who know little about the distinctions between and uses of the products they are trying to sell. It doesn't matter, though, what your customer base involves. The fact is you are likely to make exactly the same mistakes in dealing with your customers as happen in your customer service horror stories. The only way to manage your customers is to be aware of these pitfalls, and do something about it. Do it regularly and do it consistently. It's a chore. It needs organization. But it is worth it. You are in competition – this is an opportunity to differentiate yourself, because the fact is, most people will get it wrong.

I won't explicitly list what goes into doing it right, as it would turn out to be a simple inverse of doing it wrong, plus going the extra mile, but instead I will remember a few instances of my experience. The restaurant owner who, the first time we returned after a year's absence not only commented that we were sitting at the same table, but that we were sitting the other way around. The postmaster who noticed after I'd left the post office that he'd charged me too much for the parcel I'd taken in, and gave me the difference back next time I went in. The hospital we rang to ask where in the town we were visiting there would be a chemist open on a Sunday to get some medicine for our child. There wasn't one, she said, but come in here and I'll get you some. And she did – for free. The promotional products company that noted my need for a quick turnaround for a course I was giving. Not only did she tell her supplier that the order was needed for a conference (which gave it a higher priority), but she brought the pens round personally to make sure they arrived on time. And so on.

Customer values

Being nice to people can be hard work. We are all tempted sometimes to say 'I can't be bothered' and not try with a customer. But it is a salutary exercise to work out that customer's lifetime value before being so casual with them. The lifetime value is the amount of money you might expect that customer to spend with you for the rest of their life, if you keep them as a customer.

For example, I might have a customer who only ever spends £100 with me. It's trivial. He comes one day when I'm tired and I'm overloaded with other work and I tell him where he can stick his £100. A little later, when my brain is working again, I think. It might only be £100, but on average he deals with us once a month. Let's say, if we're lucky, that he could continue doing this for another twenty years. Okay – I've not just thrown away £100, I've thrown away £24,000. That's not so funny.

Whose values

When dealing with customers, always ensure that it is their value system that is used to determine what is appropriate to give and withhold. A classic example of this was when a major airline decided to save money by not providing complimentary nuts in First Class. The story made the news, and within the first few days they had received at least a hundred complaints from First Class customers, many saying that they would look at moving to other airlines. It wasn't that these people were dying for free nuts, but that they felt (considering the very large fares they were paying) that the airline was treating them shabbily. A moment's calculation showed that the lifetime value of a single customer was likely to be more than a whole year's worth of nuts. The nuts were reinstated.

Dealing with the competition

The need to differentiate yourself is one aspect of managing your competitors, but there are others. Of course there are some quite extreme schools of competition management. Organized crime, for example, sometimes feels that literally eliminating the opposition is a very practical business strategy. Yet this is not an option that is open to many of us, nor is it necessarily the best approach.

The biggest hurdle to overcome in managing the competition is accepting that they can be right and you can be wrong. Learning from your competitors seems a natural enough trick, but it is surprising how often stubborn loyalty and short-sightedness can result in collapse. Information is an important component here – if you don't know what your competitor is doing, you can't react – but so is an objective assessment of the relative merits of the competitor's products and services. You can't succeed for long just by copying. It isn't enough to find the good parts and duplicate them. But you can do a great deal by making sure that you change where you are inferior and actually build on the competitor's approach, not just follow it slavishly. Bring in the creativity techniques introduced in Chapter 5 and make a real difference.

An essential tool in managing the competition is talking to them. If you can establish good communications with your competitors you are much more likely to benefit. This doesn't mean spying on them. Industrial espionage might bring short-term gains, but doesn't build long-term advantage. But moving the competitors into a sort of alliance can benefit everyone. This isn't a question of establishing a cartel, which is bad for customers and potentially illegal. You can be in genuine competition, but still help each other out. A good example of this happening is in consulting. Two firms of consultants may well be in head-to-head competition for a particular contract, but when one has won it, the other would have no problem in helping out and sharing the profit. If you can get into a position like this with some of your competitors everyone is likely to benefit. Many businesses find themselves in a position where they have to take on more work than they can handle – by managing the competition appropriately the customer gets their results, thus improving your reputation, while the competitor also gets a slice of the action and is liable to pass excess business your way. Everybody wins.

WE ARE NOT ALONE

Know thine enemy

Step 1   *Take your personal portfolio. Pick an item which you are already involved in to some extent.*

Step 2   *Consider who your competitors are in this arena. Bear in mind, for example, if you are doing work for a large company your competitors could be both inside and outside the company.*

Step 3   *Jot down just what you know about your competitors. How does it compare with what you know about your employers and your suppliers or partners? What could you do to find out more?*

Result   *We are often more comfortable applying the concept of competition to a large business than we are to our personal portfolios. The fact is, though, that in almost any line of business you will have competitors, potential and active, who you should (but probably don't) know a lot about.*

Outside in

Managing by influence.
Suppliers, partners, customers and competitors.
Lifetime value.

In this chapter we have completed the survey of your management scope. We have seen how it is possible to manage by influence, rather than the often illusory concept of control. This will prove invaluable when dealing with externals – suppliers, partners, customers and competitors. Now it is time to return to your most central focus – yourself. We previously looked at your dream occupations, mapping out a portfolio for the future. To bring everything together, it is time to look at how that portfolio can and must change.

12 Road map to the future

key concept

Managing with constant change, becoming an internal expert, managing yourself.

Preview

- Change may frighten you or thrill you, but it needs to be part of your accepted way forward.
- Helping others to manage change is part of the role of the chameleon manager.
- Your employment dreams will change. Key strands will last for major sections of your career; available work and maturing experience tip the balance.
- Reviewing your aims and skill base.
- The role of a mentor.
- Managing your dreams.
- Flashes, links and wells – creativity, communication and knowledge.
- Making it happen.

Change – the final frontier

Most of us thrive on a balance of change and stability. We don't like total stagnation, but equally we don't like change to be occurring all the time. It is reassuring to have strands of continuity to make us feel safe. For at least a hundred years, though, the whole process of change has been speeding up. Changes which would once have taken a lifetime now occur in a year or two. For the chameleon manager, change has to be part of everyday life.

It is tempting to say that you should learn to love change, but there is a danger with this thought. Change is like a drug. You must use it appropriately, but it is possible to be come addicted, using the drug for the sake of it, not to effect a cure. Similarly, it is possible to become a change junkie, only happy when you are tearing things apart and rebuilding them. There is a fine, but necessary line between change for change's sake and the change of constant innovation for the sake of competitive advantage.

If there is a secret to coping with change, it is contained in the first paragraph of this section. However happy you are with change – personally, I love it – you still need some reference points, some steadfast rock to feel comfortable with while everything changes around you. If you are lucky this can include your home life. Whether or not you have this luxury, some degree of stability should be included in your portfolio. Some of your portfolio activities should be long-term strands. They might be relatively low priority, they might be more hobby than employment, but some should provide a degree of stability to keep you anchored.

Enterprising chameleons

It is not entirely coincidental that the previous section's title echoes the famous television science fiction series *Star Trek*. Both in the original series and particularly in the sequel, *The Next Generation*, there was an interesting use of stability to underline change. The whole life of the Enterprise crew was one of change and flexibility, yet as if to counter this, time and again there would be aspects of continuity, seeming to give the characters something to cling on to. Whether it is the frequent appearance of Shakespeare and classical music performances, Captain Picard's fishtank, or experiences on the holodeck set in the fictional world of film noir detectives, the Enterprise crew, chameleon managers one and all, used elements of stability to anchor their fluid existence.

Change-spotting

Step 1   *List the items in your personal portfolio. Mark all of those which are likely to have less than a year's duration. Mark any which will involve changing roles. Mark any which involve new skills. Mark any which involve implementing major change.*

Step 2   *Note what is left. Do you have any anchors running through your portfolio? Items which won't change in a big way over a few years.*

Result   *If all your items lacked change, your portfolio sounds too weak. If, on the other hand they all involved change, you may find it too much to take on. Try to introduce one or two activities which will provide you with some constancy. They don't have to be big, money-earning activities.*

Smooth change and step change

Change isn't, of course, all the same. In general a slow, steady change is easier to cope with than a sudden, step change. We have all seen a child after a year's gap and commented on how much it has changed. The parents don't notice anywhere near as much, as they have been subjected to a smooth, gradual change. Similarly, though more distressingly, an old friend seeing you after a number of years may well be shocked by ageing which you had hardly noticed.

If you want to make change without rocking the boat, the gradual approach has much to commend it. However, it isn't always the right answer. The very fact that step changes are more noticeable is not always a disadvantage. Where you want recognition for what you have done, you are much more likely to be recognized and rewarded for a step change than for a smooth one. It is the single act of valour that gets the medal much more often than a lifetime's collection of smaller braveries. If you are looking at change in yourself you may find that the gradual approach has a lot going for it. If, however, you want to sell change, a big step will generally go down better. A chancellor will always seem more impressive if he cuts taxes by 5 per cent in one blow than if he makes ten separate cuts of 0.5 per cent.

We don't always have a choice about the way change occurs, but when we do it is well worth considering the options.

Quantum change

In a (hopefully) rare burst of pedantry, I am very uncomfortable with the use of quantum change to mean a large step change. A quantum change is certainly a step, but in the physical applications that the term arose from, it is an extremely tiny step. I would put the term in the same limbo as the term 'decimate' deserves to be in. Decimation is now often used to mean a massacre, yet it has a very precise meaning, originating from a Roman punishment where one person in ten was killed. It's not that I object to change in language – far from it – but these are both unnecessary changes, which can cause confusion where two meanings exist in parallel. No one said all change is good.

Helping others with change

It may be your job to bring change to others. They will often be less open to change than you are. I was discussing change with the marketing director of a carpet manufacturer. 'Most of our employees,' he said, 'are in their fifties. The average time in the job is twenty years. These people do not want change. They have seen it all before, they just want stability.' This is a significant challenge. It can be seen all the time on the news, as groups of workers rebel at the imposition of new working practices, as communities mourn the passing of their traditional industry.

My carpet-making friend was right – such people don't go looking for change. But this does not mean that it is impossible to bring change to them. I have seen pensioners who have never used a computer in their life take to it and enjoy it. It doesn't do to underestimate what people are capable of. Yet it certainly is possible to implement change in such a way that it will be almost universally rejected. Announce from on high that change is going to happen. Tell them when and what is going to happen to them. And sit back to wait for the protest.

Effecting change with others is not a job for old, command and control management. It needs new, chameleon management. You must be prepared to share information, to tutor those who are going to undergo change as to what the options are, why you are heading in a particular direction and what it will mean for them. You need to have a mechanism not only for discussing change, but for them to influence the change. I am not saying hand over the company, but turn an inclination to destruction into a positive force for improvement.

Easier said than done? Absolutely. It is almost impossible, but if you can pull it off, you've got something that's a lot better for everyone than the old confrontations. If possible, your best hope is to turn the staff who have to change into chameleon managers. If they are doing their jobs with the same sense of contributing to a personal portfolio as you are, there's a much better chance of swinging them behind a logical decision (of course, this assumes the change you are trying to implement is logical). Yes, you will lose some who decide their portfolio takes them elsewhere, but it will be worth it in the long run.

Reviewing yourself

I have talked about your projected perfect occupations in terms of a dream, yet a dream is a very unstable entity. Dreams flow and change constantly; they are not static. Sometimes dreams are subject to sudden, apparent discontinuities (though they often appear sensible at the time). Similarly your picture of your dream portfolio will change over time. Some aspects will gradually modify. Others will have sudden, almost catastrophic, step changes. Both external and internal influences will affect how you see your desired future. You can't define your portfolio once and imagine that it will last you the rest of your working life. It will need revisiting.

It makes sense to review your aims and your skill base on a regular basis. This needn't be an onerous task. You could restrict it to once a year. A good time would be at the New

Year or on a birthday, traditional times for reviewing your progress in life. To keep the need for a review in mind, and to ensure that you have the time to complete it, schedule it into your diary - with anything that happens this infrequently, it's not enough to rely on memory alone to make it happen. While you are at it, check that your CV is up to date.

There are other occasions when a review becomes valuable. Sometimes an external influence will cause you to act. It might be the completion of a major piece of work, a promotion or being made redundant. It might be a change in family circumstances, a natural disaster or the discovery of a new passion. The important thing is not to be too rigid about your reviewing - be prepared to bring it forward if events justify it - and remember the need for a review when such a circumstance arises.

Although occasionally it can be beneficial to start from scratch, it is generally sensible to build on your previous pictures. Check your skills base. What has changed? Look through your dream activities. Are there items which aren't so important any more? Is something missing? Are the obstacles you identified still there? Use one or two of the activities in Chapter 2 to clarify your portfolio and to establish whether new obstacles have arisen.

Schedule a review

Before reading any further, get your diary and enter in it a date on which to review your portfolio. As these are early days you might like to make it in six months' time rather than a year. While you are at it, note in the same diary entry to schedule the next review date, either a year after that or at the next appropriate key date like New Year or your birthday.

Finding a mentor

There's something rather lonely about being a chameleon manager. You are redefining yourself based on your dreams and desires, which is fine, but you have few independent points of reference. Most good ideas benefit from having someone else, someone with a different viewpoint, to bounce them off. In a traditional employment framework there was the concept of a managed career, steered by a caring company in the direction which would bring out the best in you. In practice, of course, this was so much rubbish. The people developing this career path for you had neither the time nor the knowledge to make it fit well. They were considering the company's needs much more than yours. Yet losing this support from your manager or personnel or human resources (HR) professional can be unnerving. Enter the mentor.

The concept of a mentor is ideal for the chameleon manager. A mentor should be one of your peers or someone with more experience. The mentor's role is to act as a sounding board for your ideas, to reinforce what is good about them and to gently encourage you to cut out what's bad. The mentor can point you to new possibilities and help you clarify your goals. They do everything you might have expected from the old manager/HR combination, but actually deliver. What's in it for them? Your mentor is also likely to be a chameleon manager. There's a mutuality about the process that is very valuable. Being a mentor is closer to friendship than a business agreement. And most mentors will want to have their own mentors – there's an element of do as you would be done by.

Where should you get your mentor from? Only you can know the exact circumstances that make someone a good mentor, but there are a few guidelines. A mentor will often be someone who has worked in the same company as you in the past, but has moved on to bigger and better things. They can relate to your need to change, having made a change themselves. They will often be a senior manager or director (though increasingly of their own small company). They need not have any experience of the type of business you are involved in, but they will have a broad understanding of the business area. They might have been your boss in the past, or even your boss now (though you would need an exceptionally good relationship with your boss for the latter to be the case). Finally, they need to be accessible. There's no point having a mentor who doesn't return your calls and can't meet for lunch. Having a meal (or a drink) with a mentor on a regular basis is essential, as such informal contact is ideal for the type of interchange that is necessary.

Mentor shopping

Step 1   *Establish whether you already have a mentor. I didn't realize I had one until I thought about it – when I did think, it became obvious. If you have, the activity is over apart from making sure you treat them nicely and keep them in good working order.*

Step 2   *Imagine you have just got a new job, or you've a problem at work. Apart from your immediate family, who would you turn to discuss it? (I'd specifically avoid your family. They have too much to gain or lose by your decisions. A mentor needs a degree of detachment.) If there is someone, could they become a mentor? If there are several people, who best fits the picture? Once more, if you have now identified a mentor you need go no further, but jump on to the results section.*

Step 3   *If no one springs to mind immediately, resort to your little black book. A mentor does not have to be a close friend or colleague, just someone you are very comfortable talking to who is accessible and has the appropriate knowledge. It would be surprising if you couldn't find someone in the little black book who is appropriate. Test the water. Don't plunge in and say 'will you be my mentor?' They will probably move away and point out that they are happily married. Instead ask to talk through a business problem or decision, particularly if it's about your personal portfolio, and see how they react. You may need a few tries to hit the right person, but you will know when you have.*

Result   *This is one of the most important activities in the book. Without a mentor it will be difficult to make it as a chameleon manager. Note, by the way, that there is no mystical rule limiting you to one mentor. Having said that, you may have a whole bunch of people who you use as a sounding board for different aspects of your work, but the chances are that only one will be a full-scale mentor. Note also that* *the mentor role will probably shift over time. One inevitable aspect of taking on a personal portfolio is that you and your work will change. This may well involve a change in mentor too.*

Being a mentor

Eventually, often unconsciously, you are likely to become a mentor yourself. The role may not be consciously acknowledged, yet you could become the person someone else turns to when they need to talk about the direction of their career. Don't be tempted to sideline them. Remember that one of the big differences between the chameleon management style and conventional management is more consideration for a win-win position. Seeing someone else develop has often been regarded with a mixture of jealously and concern that the other person will take over or take the lead. This seems a very counterproductive approach. And if the other person ends up your boss, or a source of a work, which would you rather had happened on the way there: that they knew you to be supportive and helpful, or evasive and destructive?

Managing your dreams

If you can dream – and not make dreams your master.
(Rudyard Kipling, in *If*)

If there is one thing this book has encouraged you to do it is to clarify your dreams and do something about them. The Kipling quote is very apt. You need to be able to dream, to lift your head above the everyday and to see what is possible, perhaps improbable but possible for you. At the same time, you cannot afford to have your dream become your master. An obsession with your dream, sacrificing all else, will make you a very unattractive person, probably ruin your private life, and in the end is more likely to end up with you becoming bitter and unfulfilled rather than happy. Your dream portfolio should set your direction, should be a constant reminder, but should never be in total control. For once, the chameleon manager does need to resort to management. In your relationship with them, the dream is the leader, but you are the manager.

Flashes, links and wells

A recurring theme throughout this book has been the need for creativity, communication and knowledge. In my mid-twenties, when the impetus of education and finding a job had settled and I first seriously asked what I wanted to do with my life, I realized that practically everything I enjoyed doing centred around these three key elements. I'm lucky in this respect. But whether or not they turn you on, they remain at the centre of chameleon management.

Does it seem that the emphasis is too strong? Surely there is a need for all those good, old management strengths like planning, monitoring and decision-making? Absolutely. Yet what we see here is somewhat similar to the distinction between leadership and management, or between school physics and university physics. In physics at school level there are a whole set of rules and laws that have to be remembered and recovered parrot fashion. At university it seems more that these rules can be derived from a small number of underlying principles. Fully understand the principles (not by any means a trivial matter) and you can produce the rest whenever you like.

The leader works by setting direction and principle – again, all the manager's checks and balances can be deduced from these, but they don't need to be set out in detail. In fact, they can't afford to be, as the fast-changing world means that the rules would have to be rewritten every week, but the principles remain and continue to work. The same argument applies to the chameleon manager. Given your direction from your personal portfolio and the principles of creativity, communication and knowledge, you can derive practically any of the management skills you might need to survive and thrive.

If you aren't happy with the proposition that any management activity can be brought down to some combination of creativity, communication and knowledge, try it out. Take a management practice, skill or activity. Analyse what underlies it. Where did it come from, what is it based on? If you still can't make the link, drop me an e-mail (easiest done from the Web site, http://www.cul.co.uk/chameleon) and I'll give you my opinion.

Are you going to do anything?

In all but one sense, this book will have been a waste of time if you do nothing as a result of reading it. Luckily there is a single positive outcome even if you take no action at all. By buying it, you will have contributed to my dreams, my chameleon existence. But surely that isn't enough? If you resisted the activities, go back and do them. If you have undertaken the activities, if you've identified your dream state, think carefully about what you are doing by taking no action. You are saying that your dreams are all very well, but there's no point trying to attain them. At the risk of sounding like one of those irritating little books full of smug aphorisms, unless you try to make something happen you haven't much hope.

I can't put across pleading in type. It all comes across at the same, comfortable monotone. Yet that's what I'm doing. Asking you to think about the implications of becoming a chameleon manager. Why not try to make something, something more of what you've got?

The choice is yours.

Index

Resources for the Chameleon Manager

http://www.cul.co.uk/chameleon

The Chameleon Manager web site is part of the Creativity Unleashed Limited site – a superb source of resources for the chameleon manager

- Follow up the book – new developments and links from the Chameleon Manager
- Books – Recommendations and direct access to the world's biggest online bookshops for business, creativity and science fiction
- Software – free creativity software to download
- Consultancy – training and facilitation in business creativity
- Links – relevant web sites around the world

and more...

http://www.cul.co.uk/chameleon